Impressions *of* Italy

FROM MILAN TO ROME

A TRAVEL PHOTO ART BOOK

LAINE CUNNINGHAM

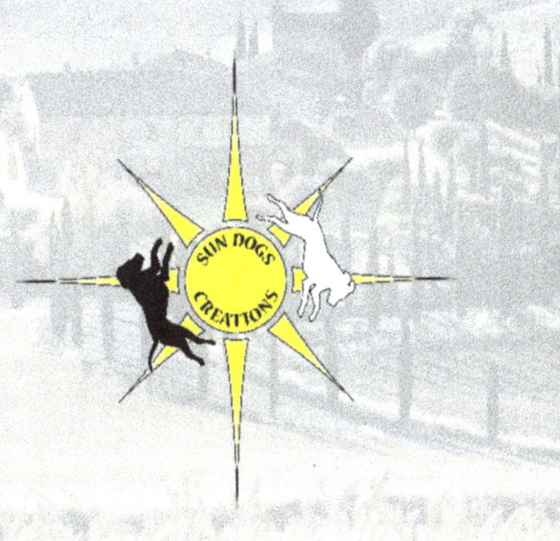

Impressions of Italy
From Milan to Rome
A Travel Photo Art Book

Published by Sun Dogs Creations
Changing the World One Book at a Time
Print ISBN: 9781946732811

Cover Design by Angel Leya

Copyright © 2018 Laine Cunningham

THE TRAVEL PHOTO ART SERIES

Bikes of Berlin

Necropolises of New Orleans I & II

Ruins of Rome I & II

Ancients of Assisi I & II

Panoramas of Portugal

Nuances of New York

Glimpses of Germany

Impressions of Italy

Utopia of the Unicorn

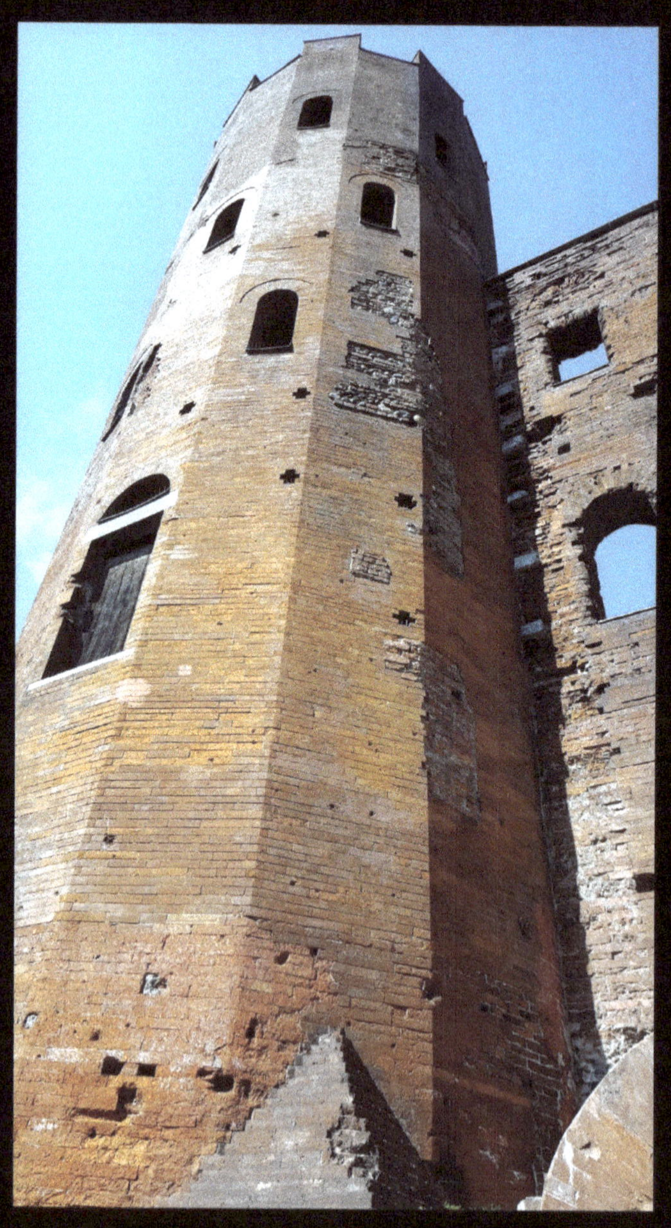

CHORUS

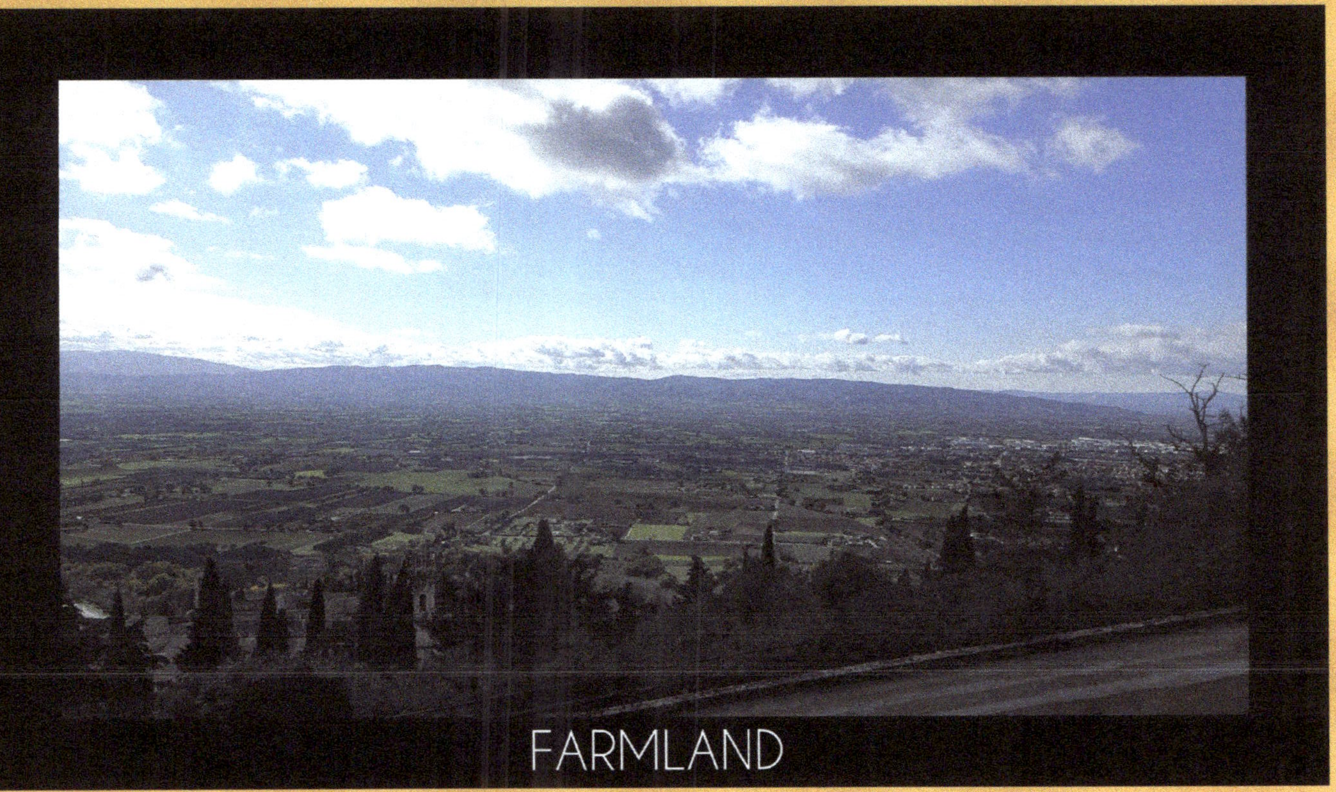

FARMLAND

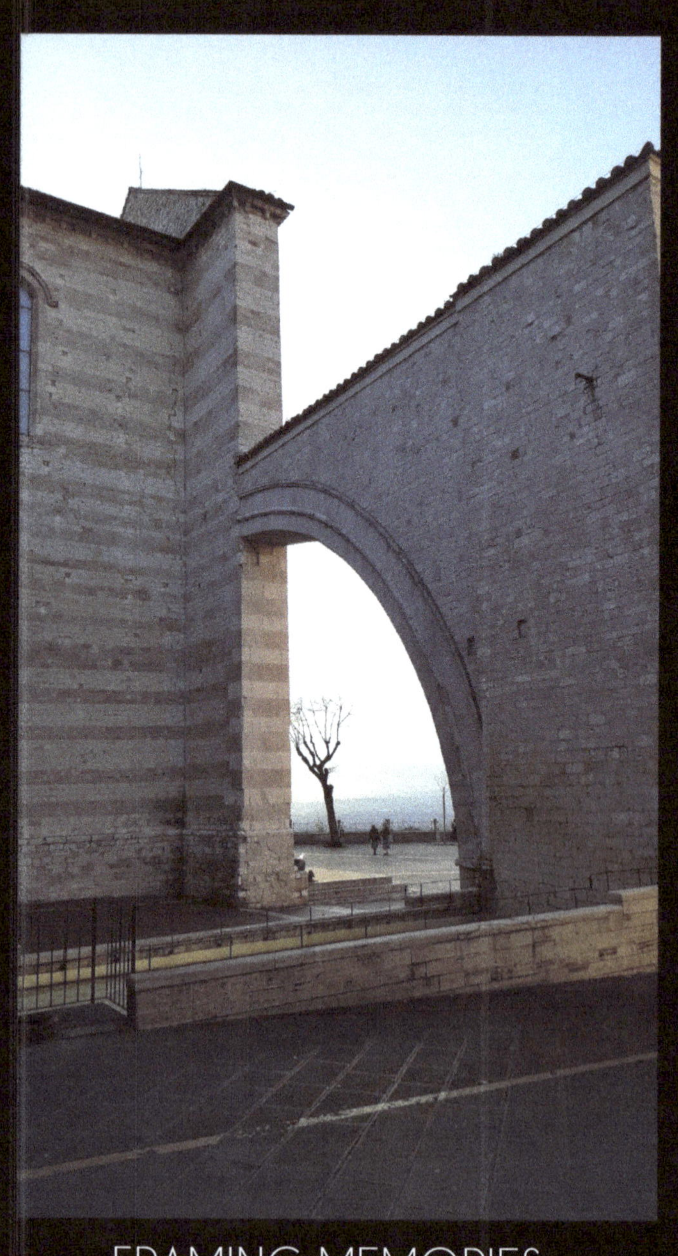
FRAMING MEMORIES

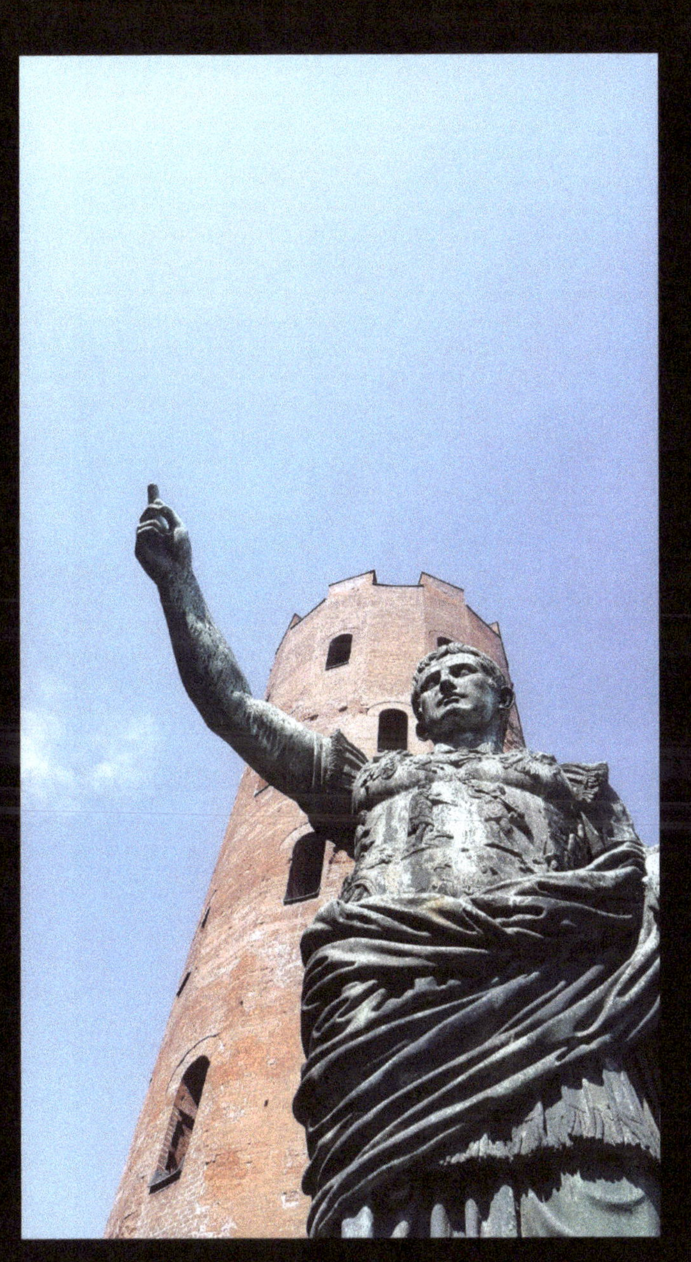

HARK

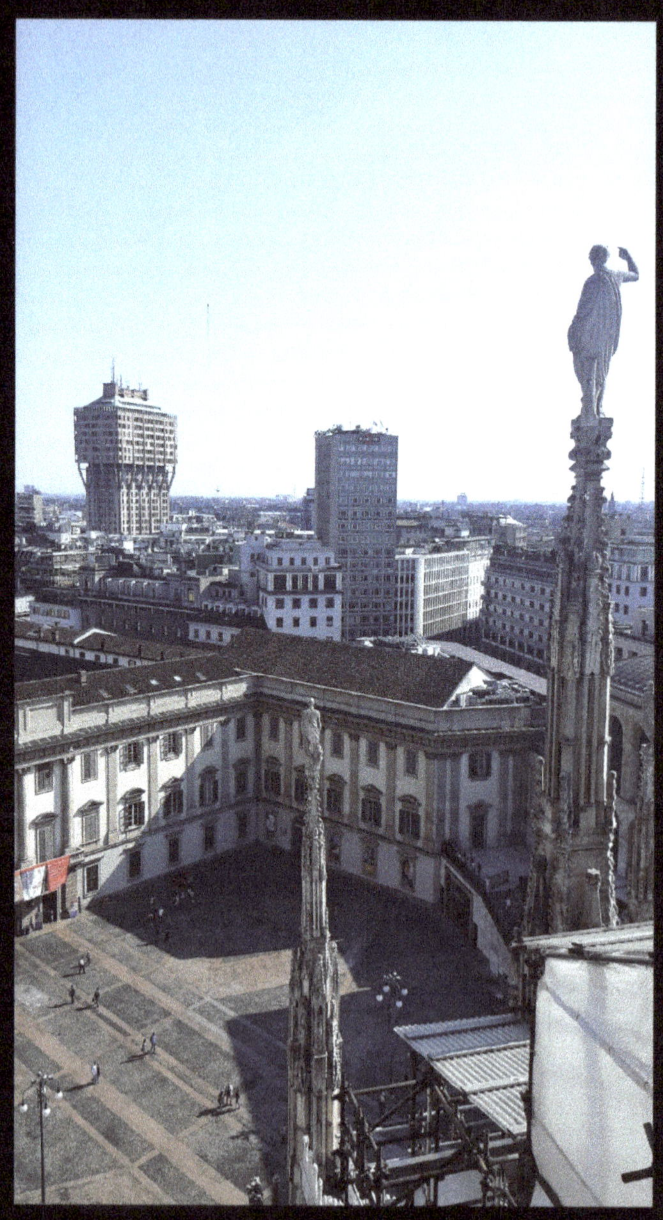

INTERSECT

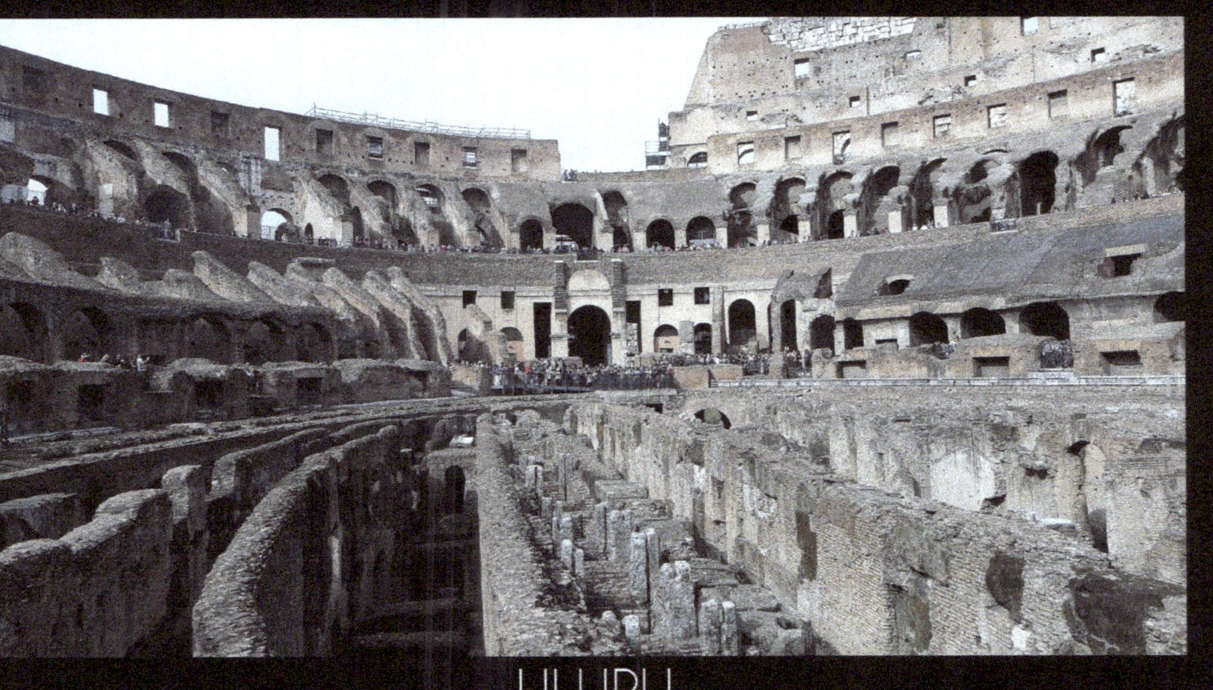
ULURU

ENFORCE

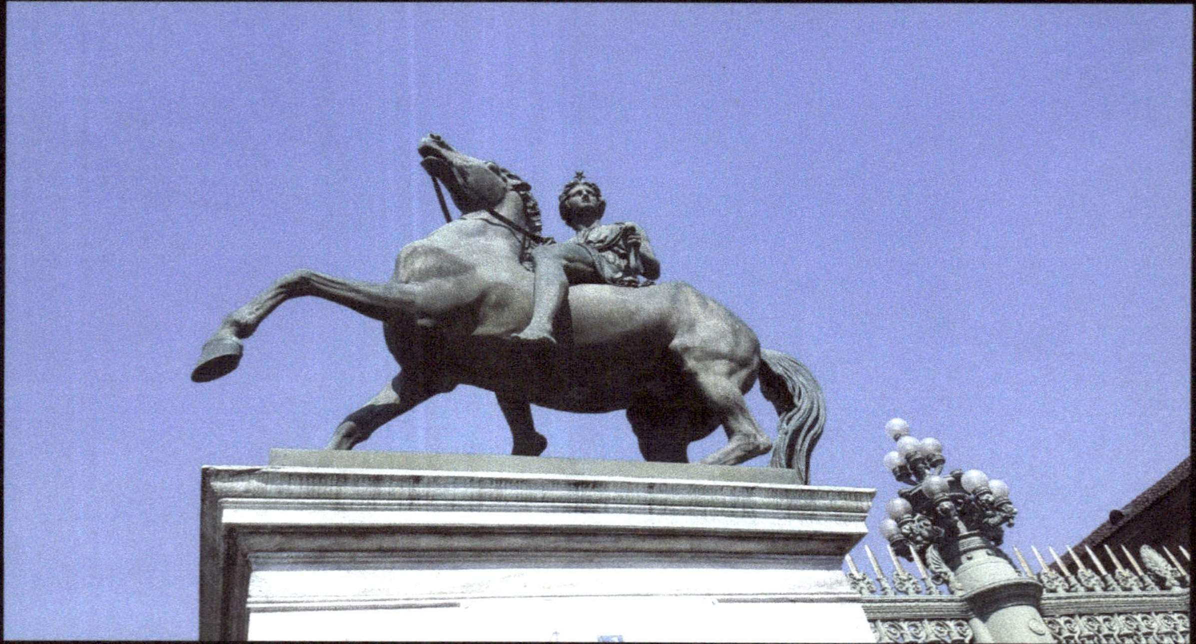

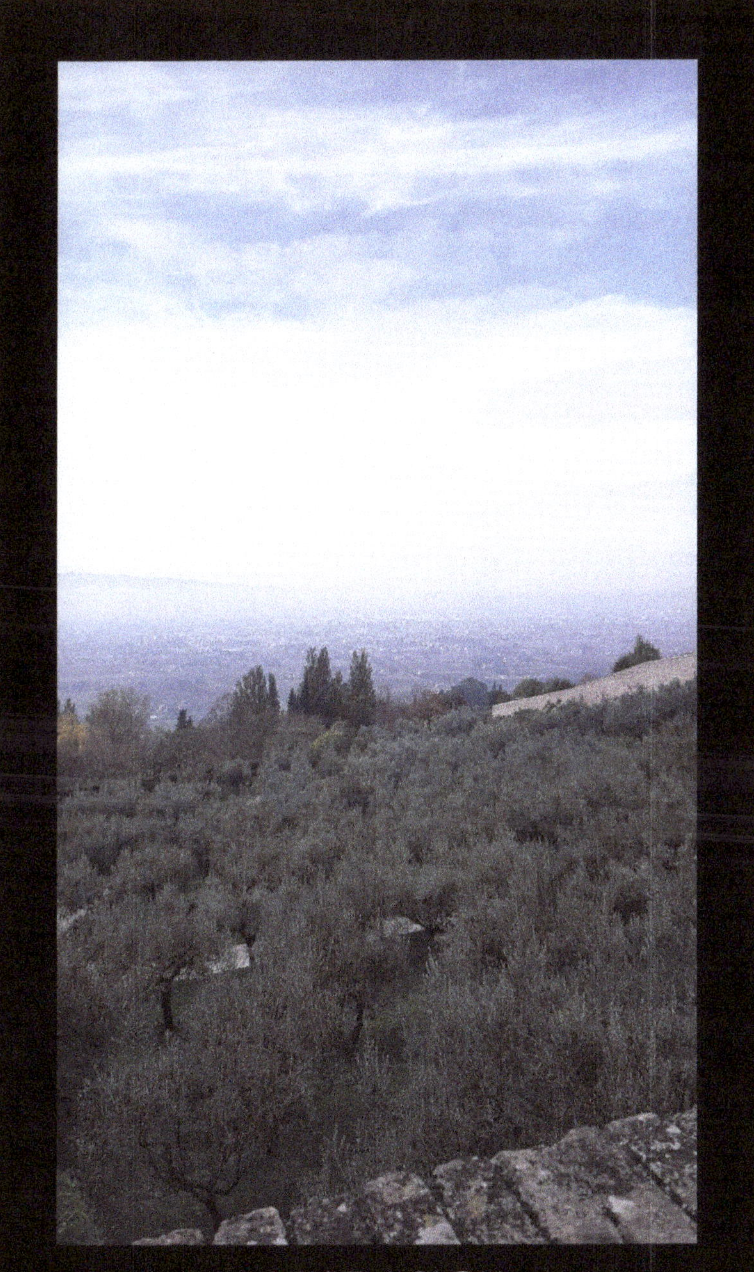
MISTY SIGH

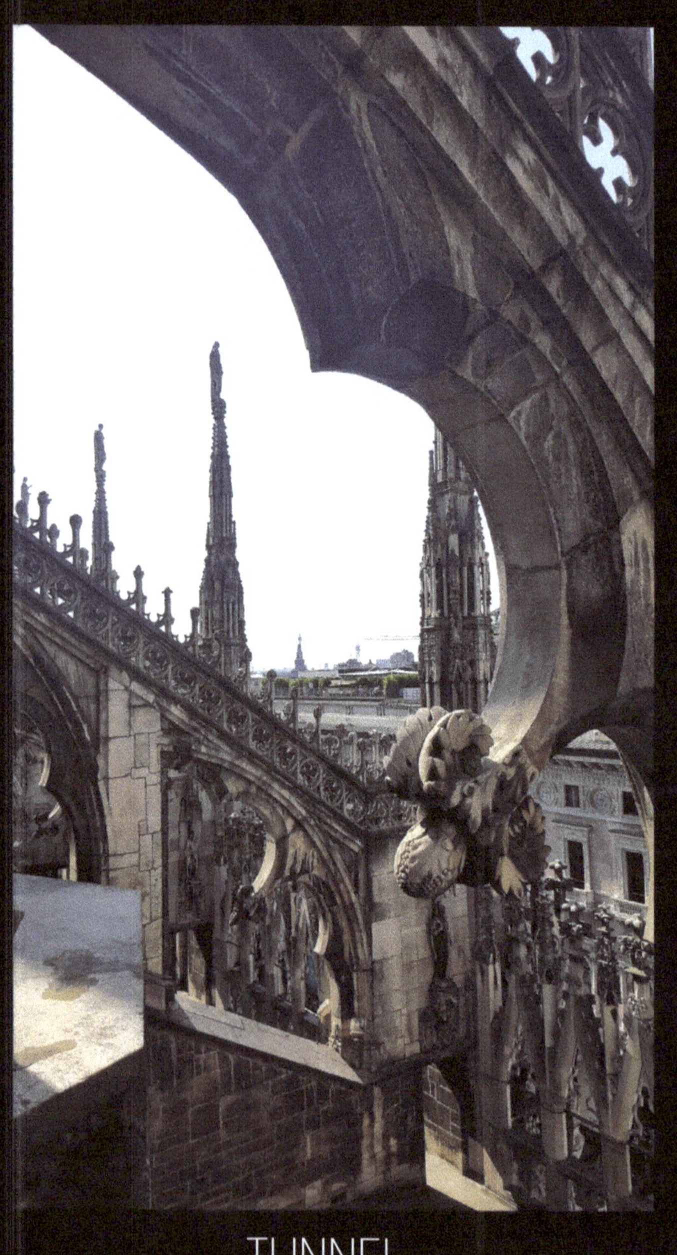

TUNNEL

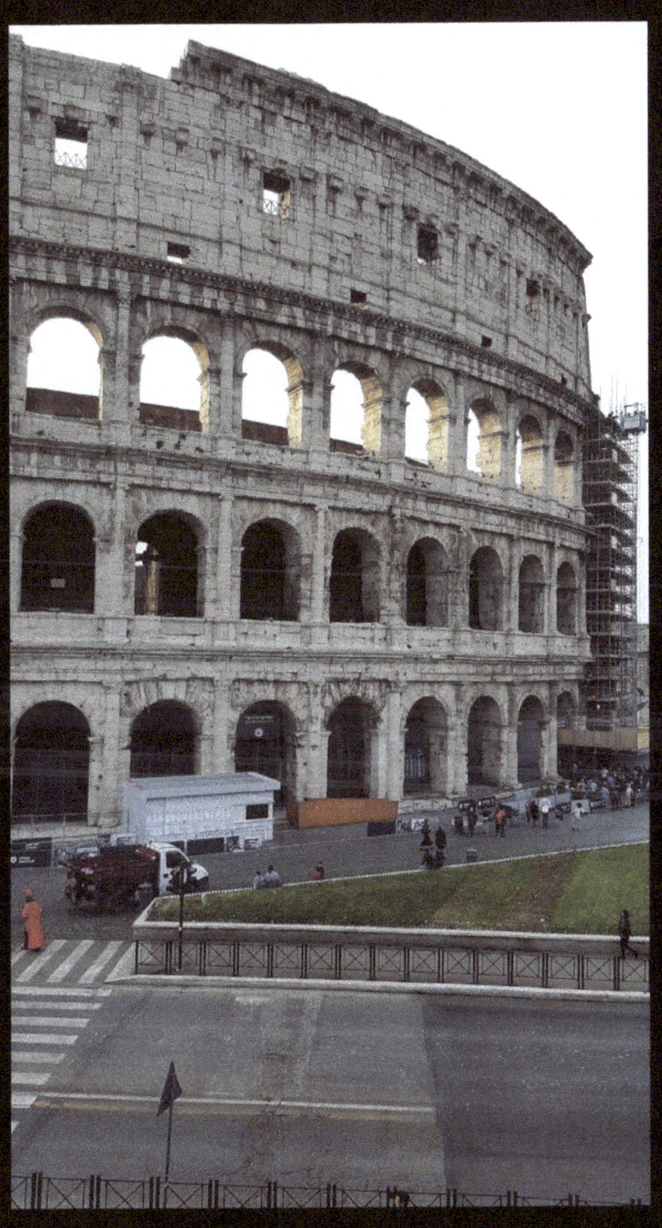

LAYER CAKE

LAND BEYOND

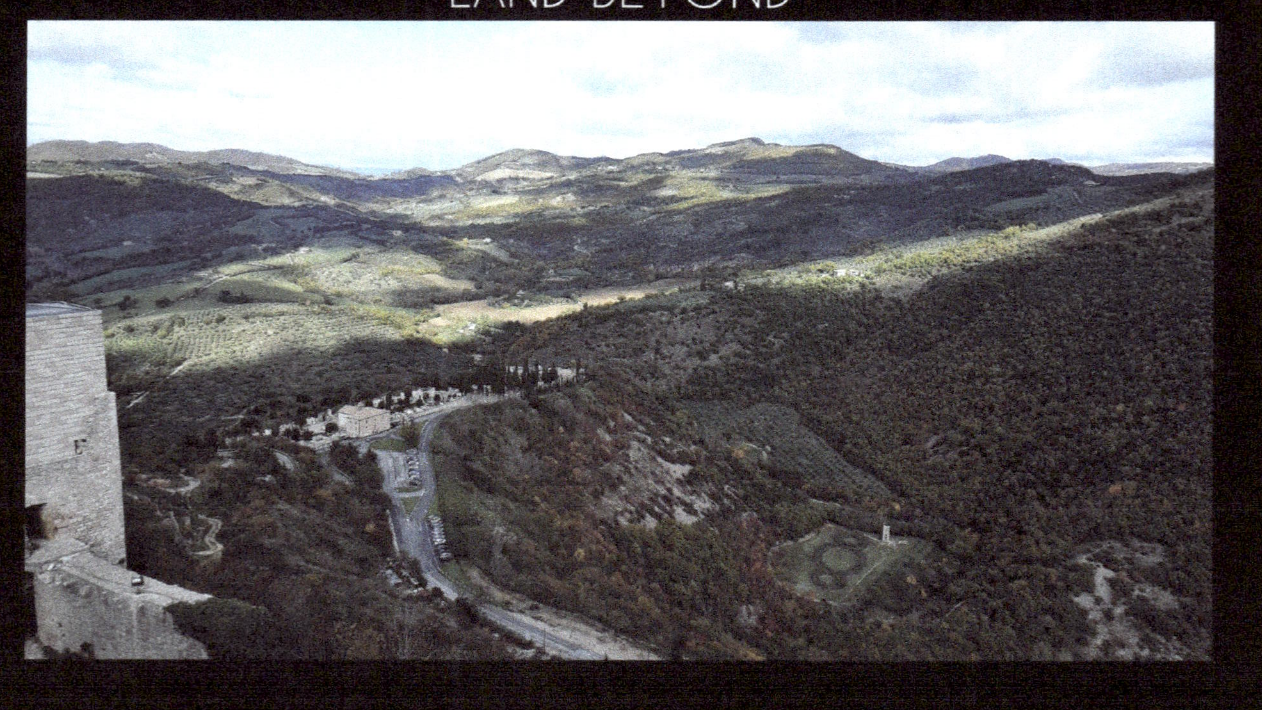

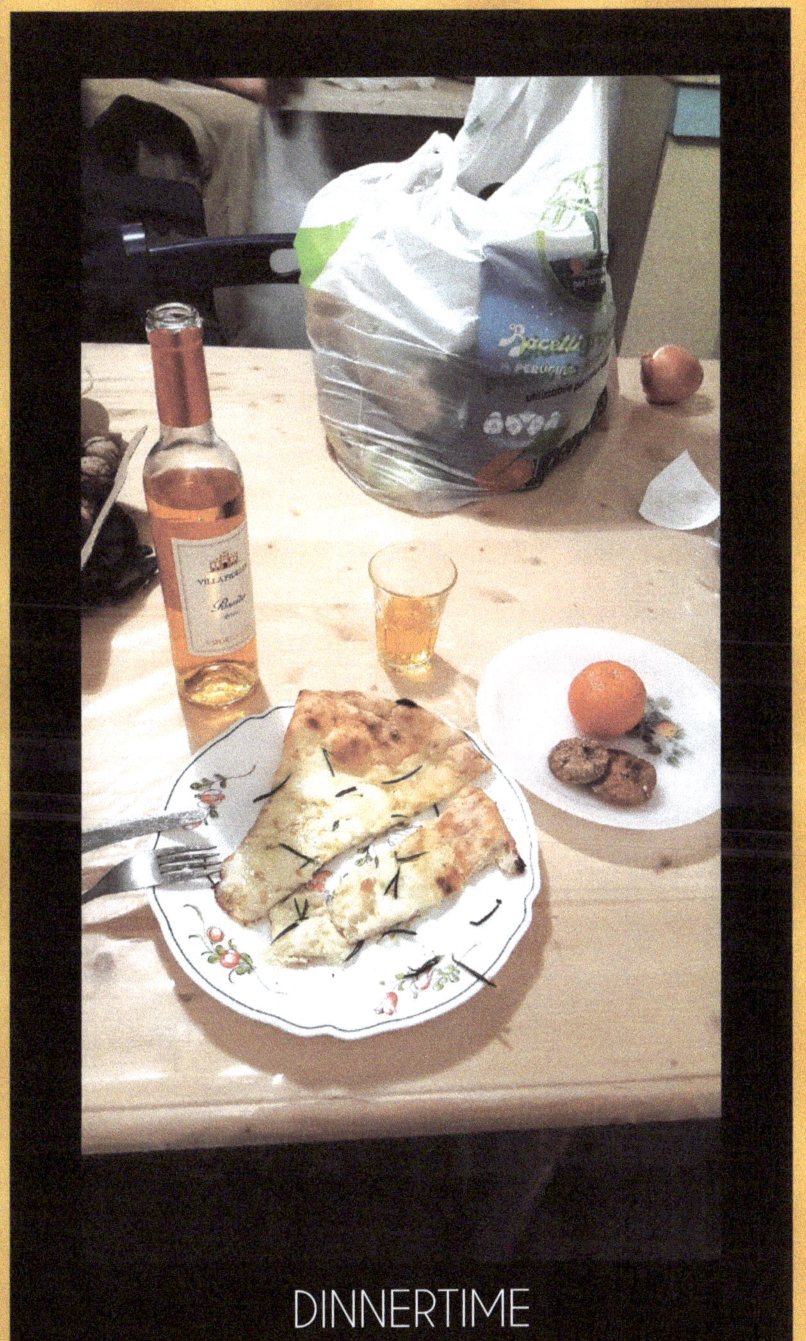

DINNERTIME

PLAYTIME

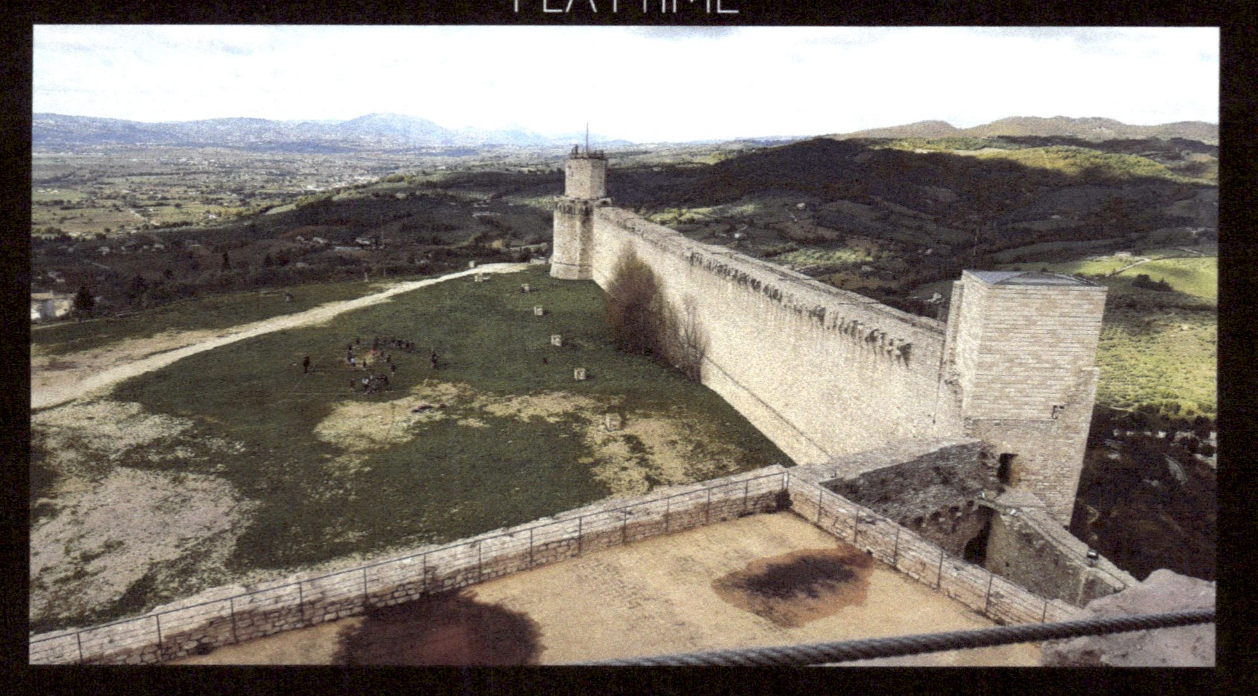

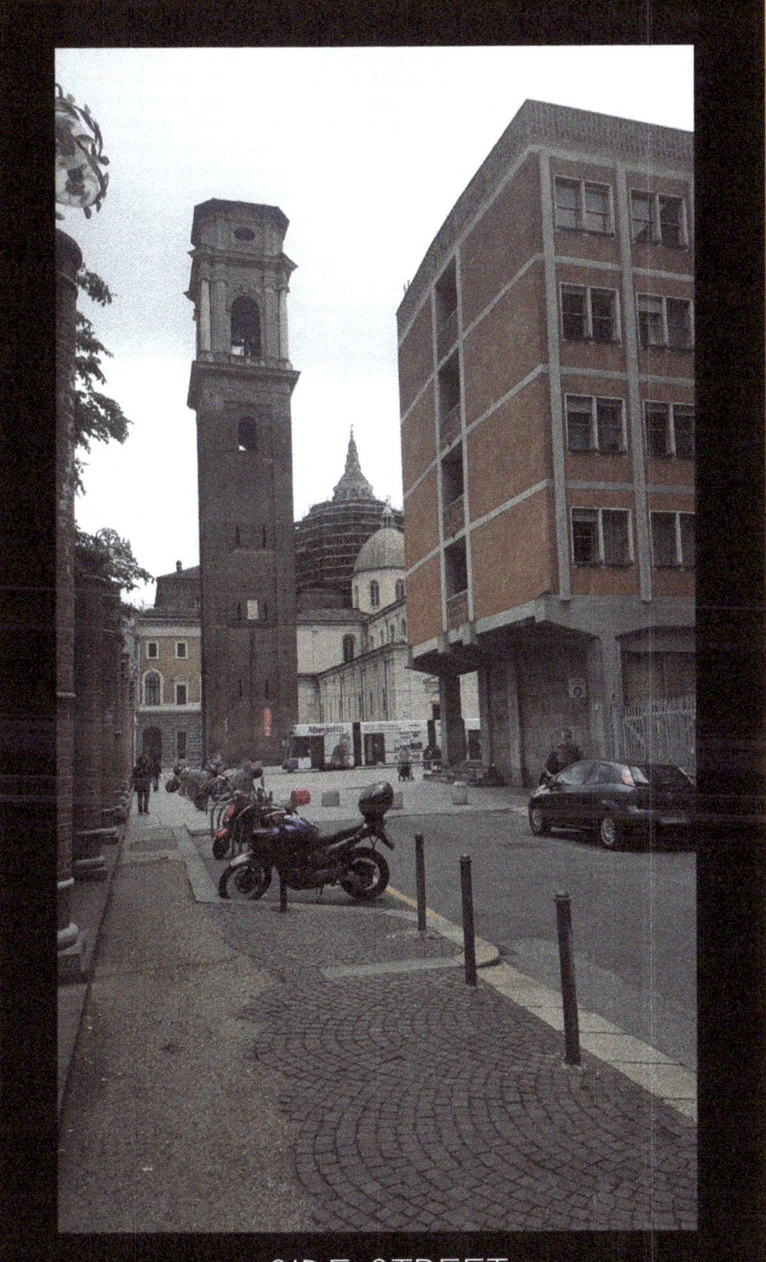

SIDE STREET

TINY VALLEY

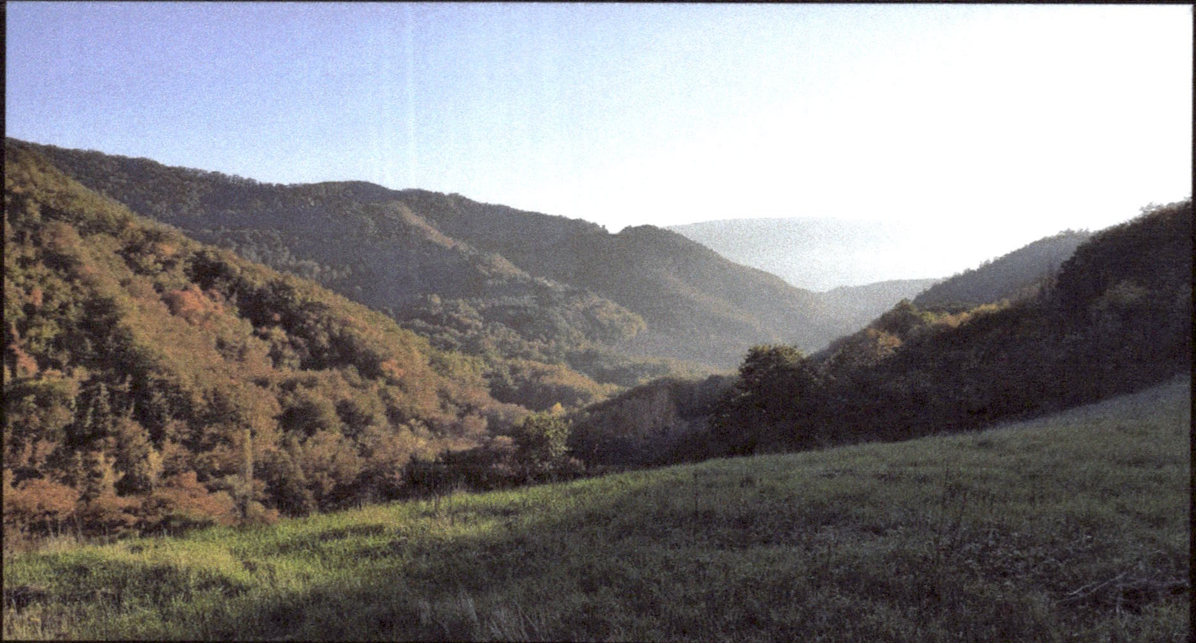

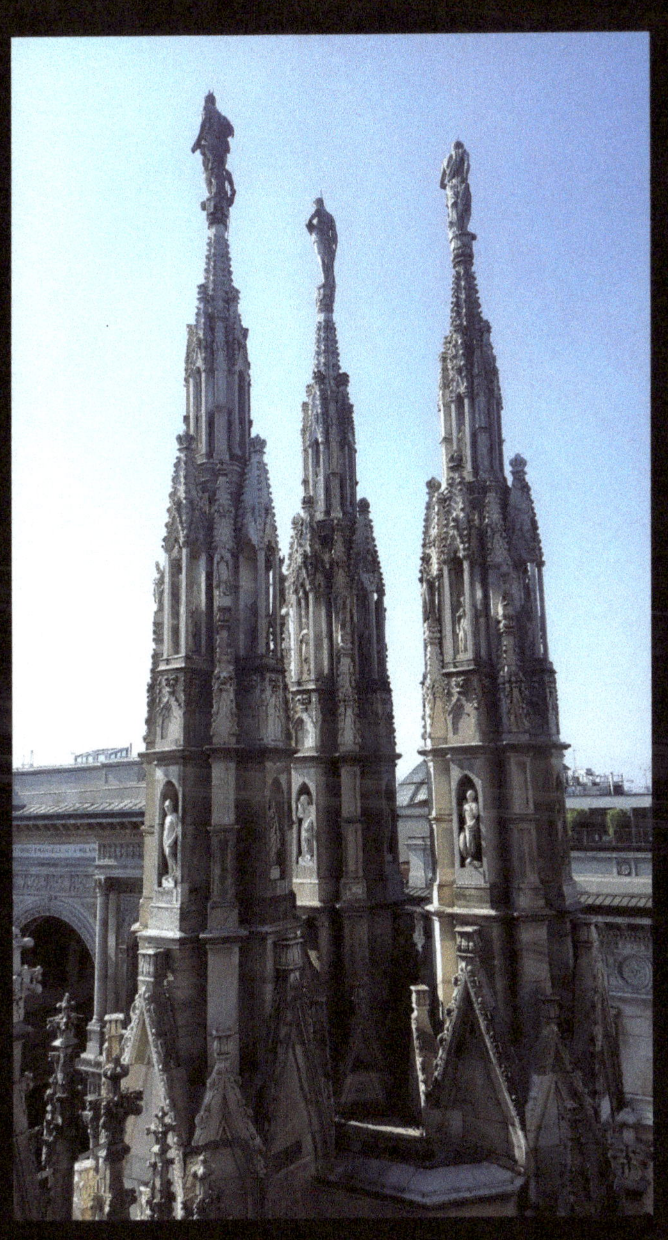

TREES

FESTIVAL DAY

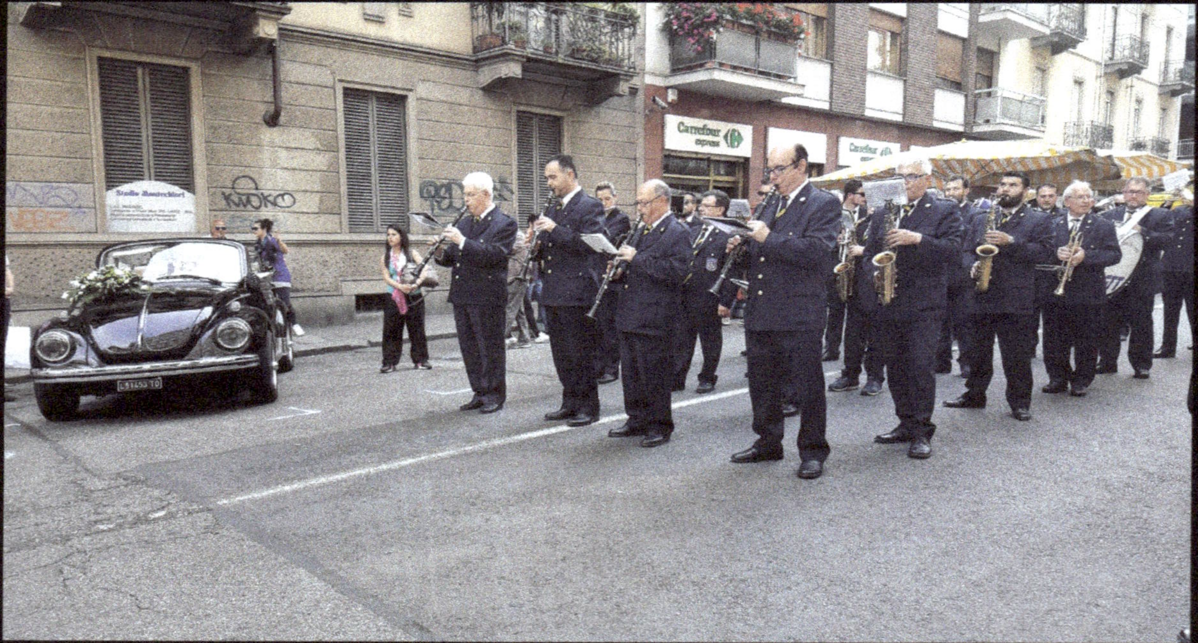

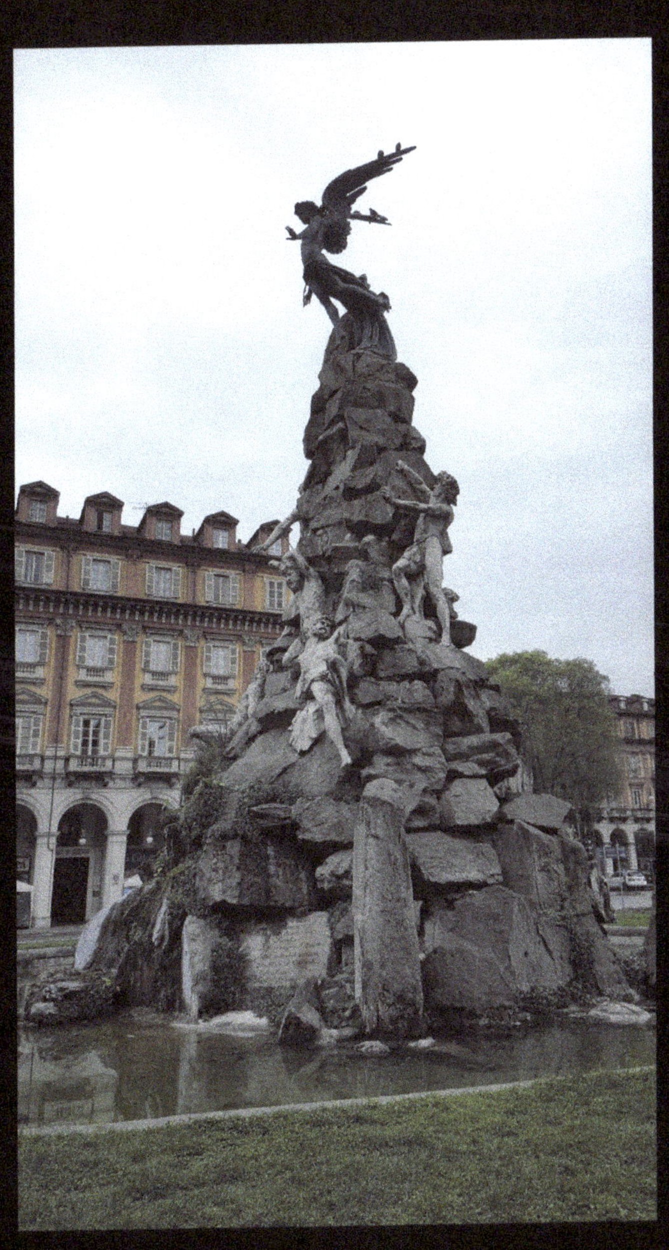

DARK ANGEL

ENTANGLED

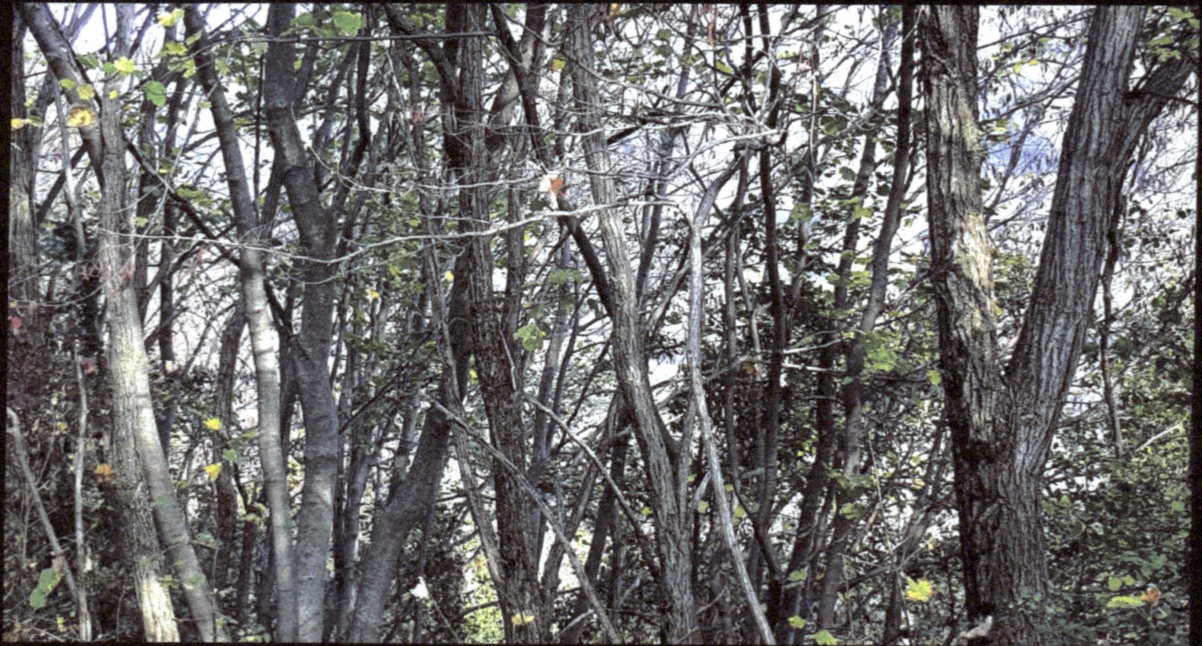

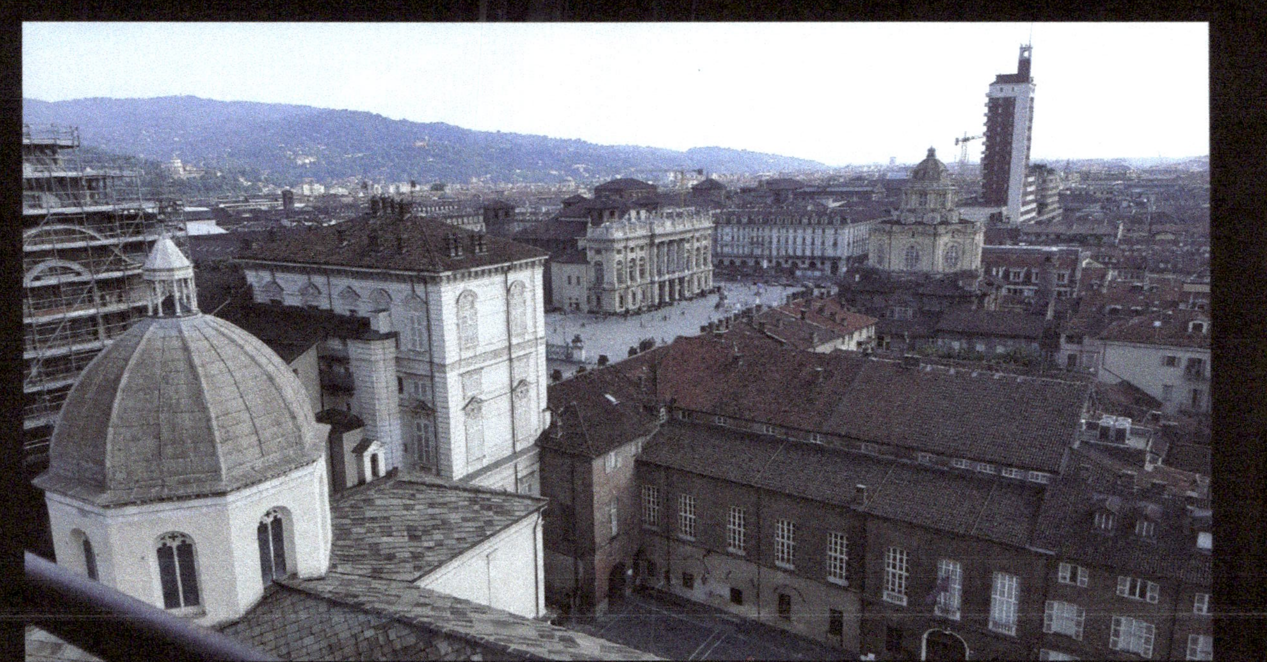

HATS AND CAPS

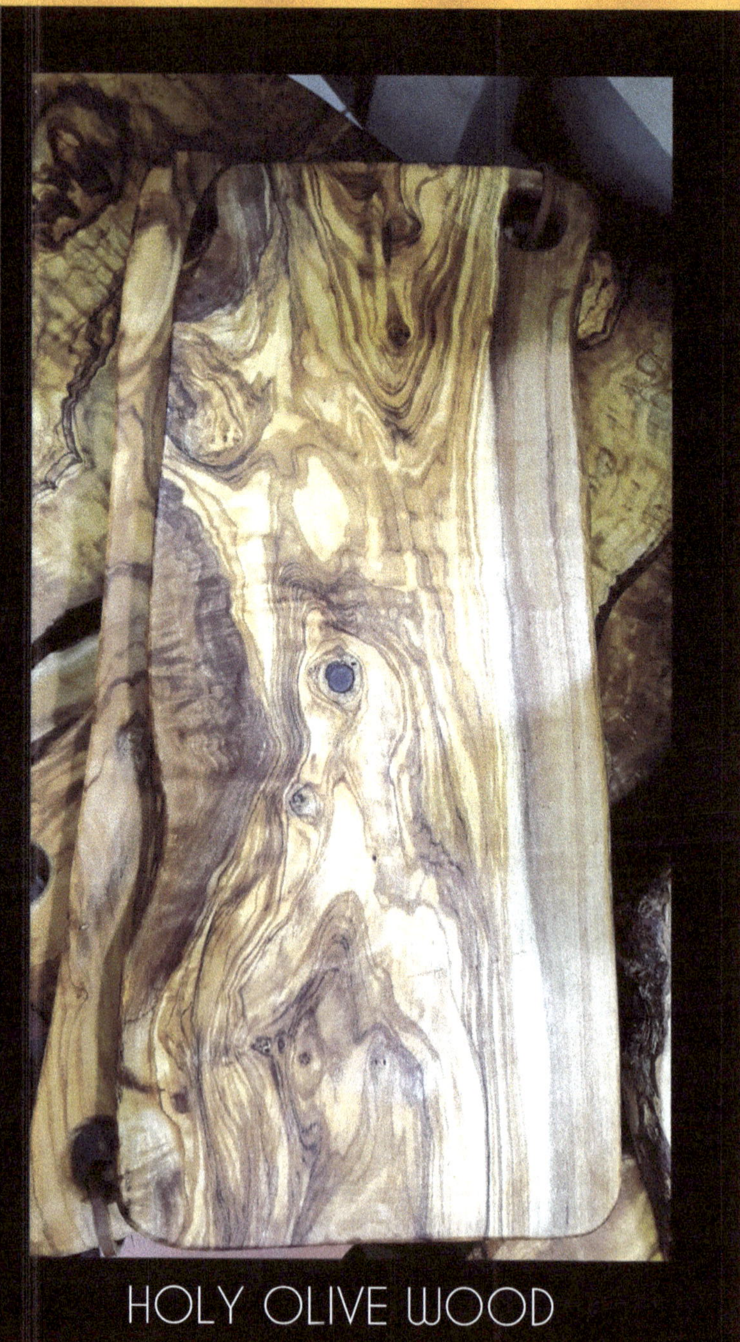

HOLY OLIVE WOOD

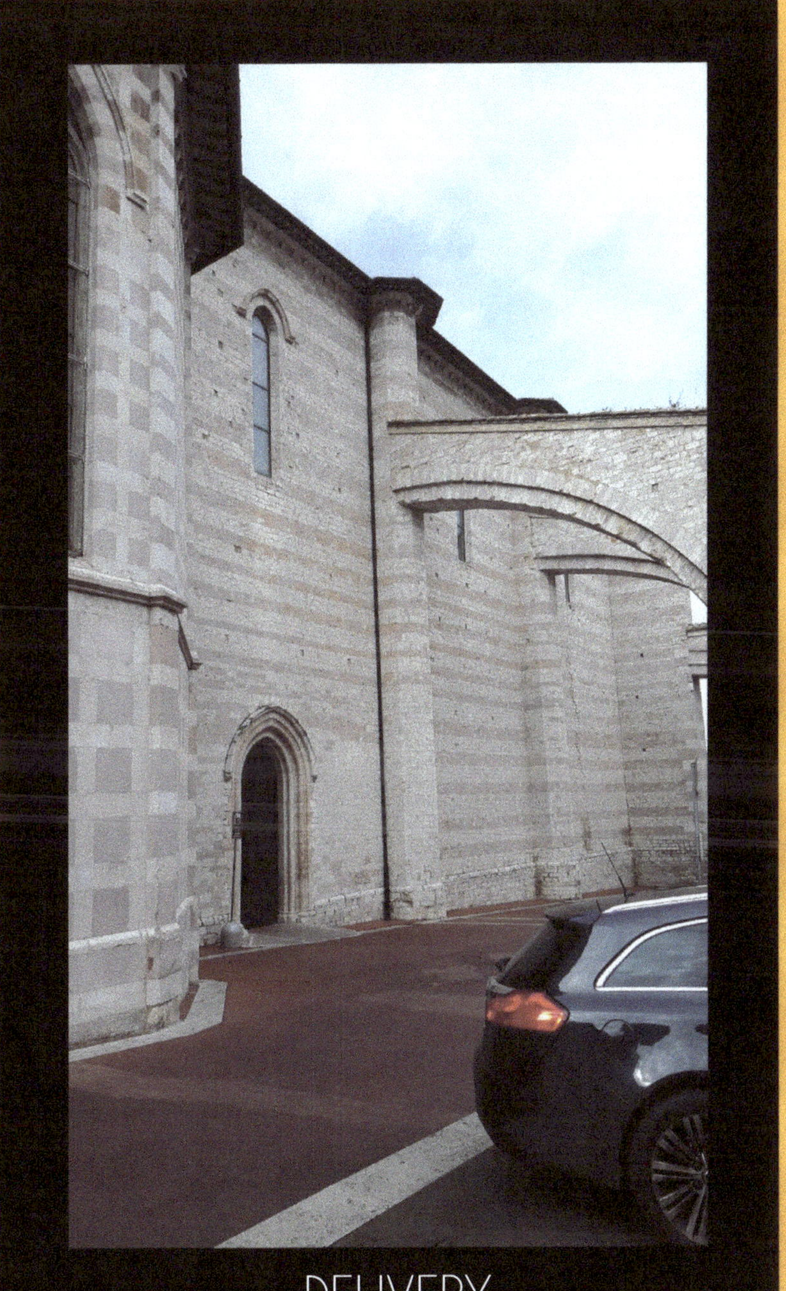
DELIVERY

BEACHFRONT PROPERTY

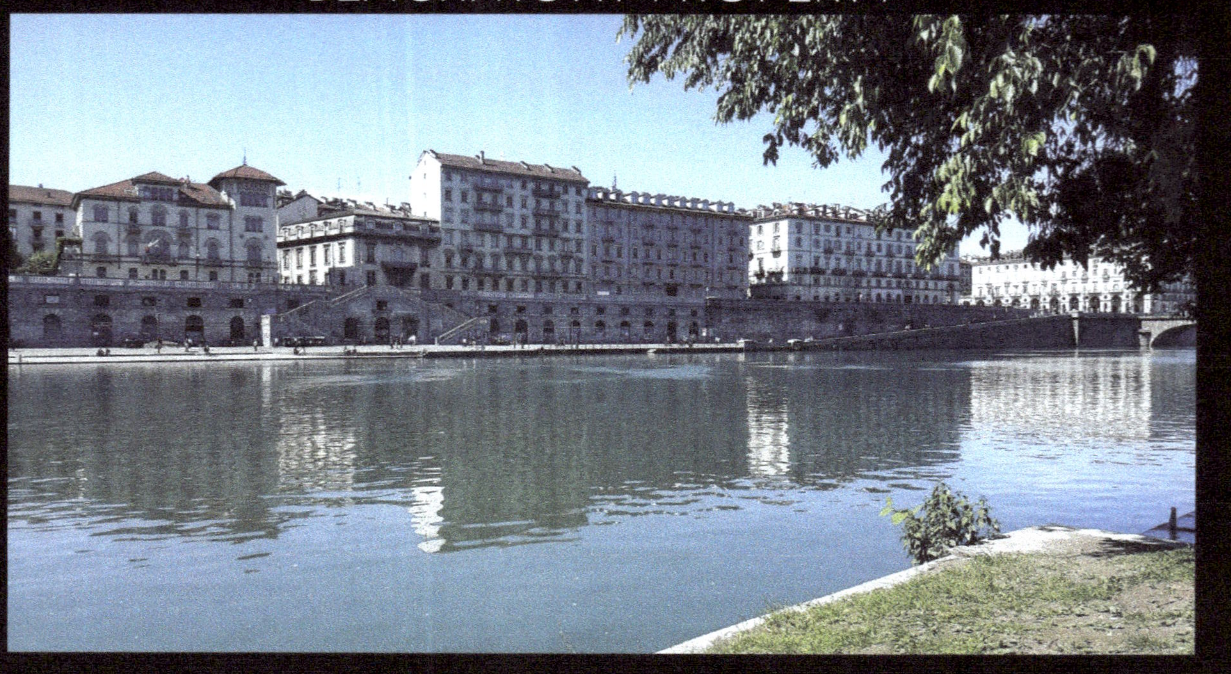

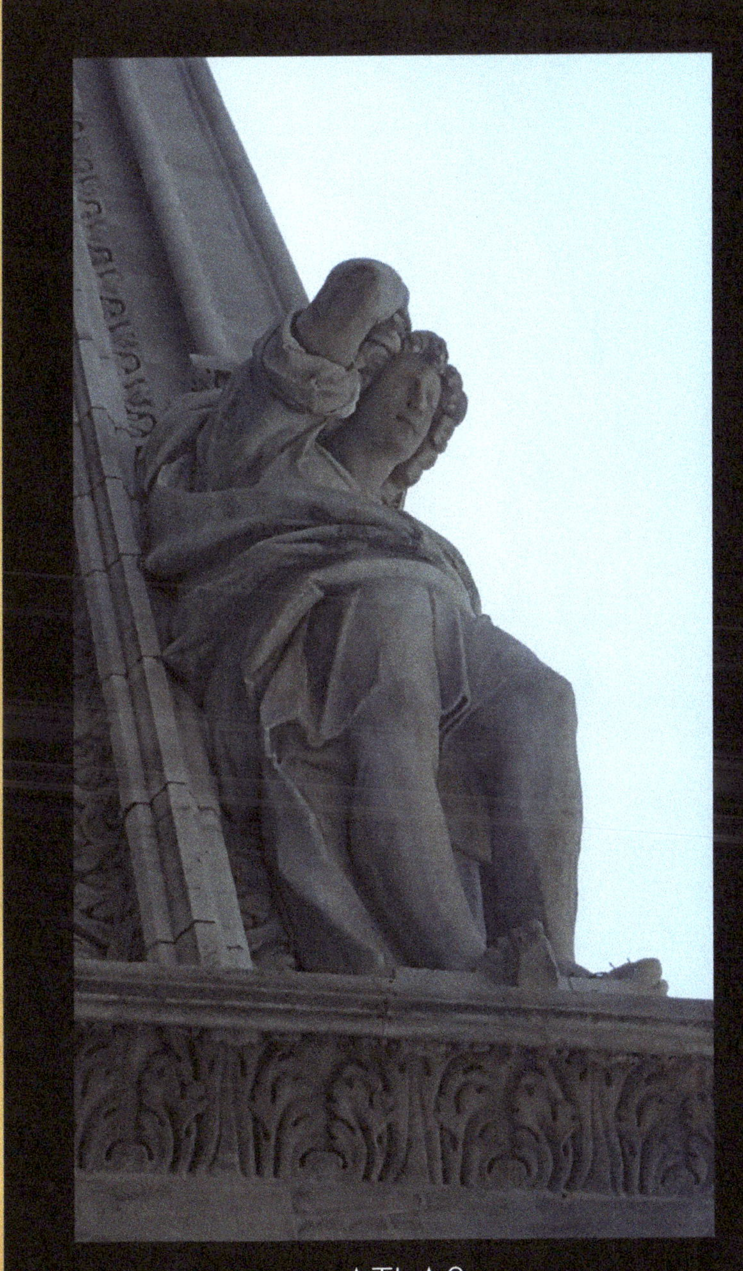

ATLAS

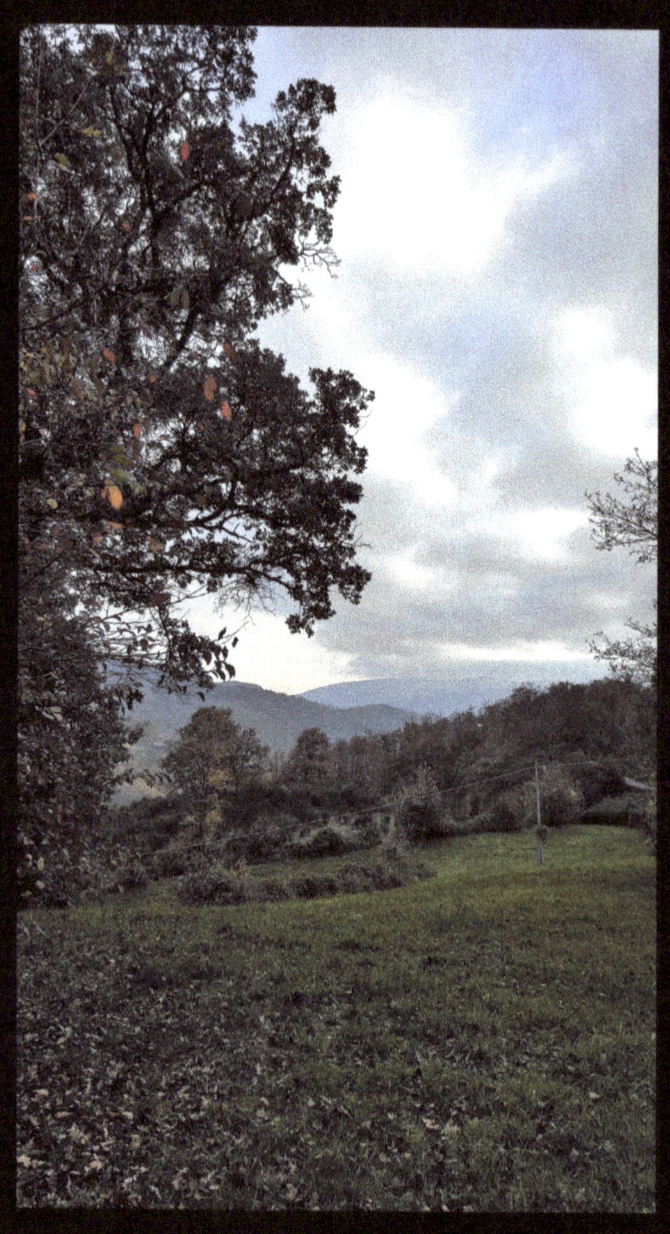

COUNTRY KEYHOLE

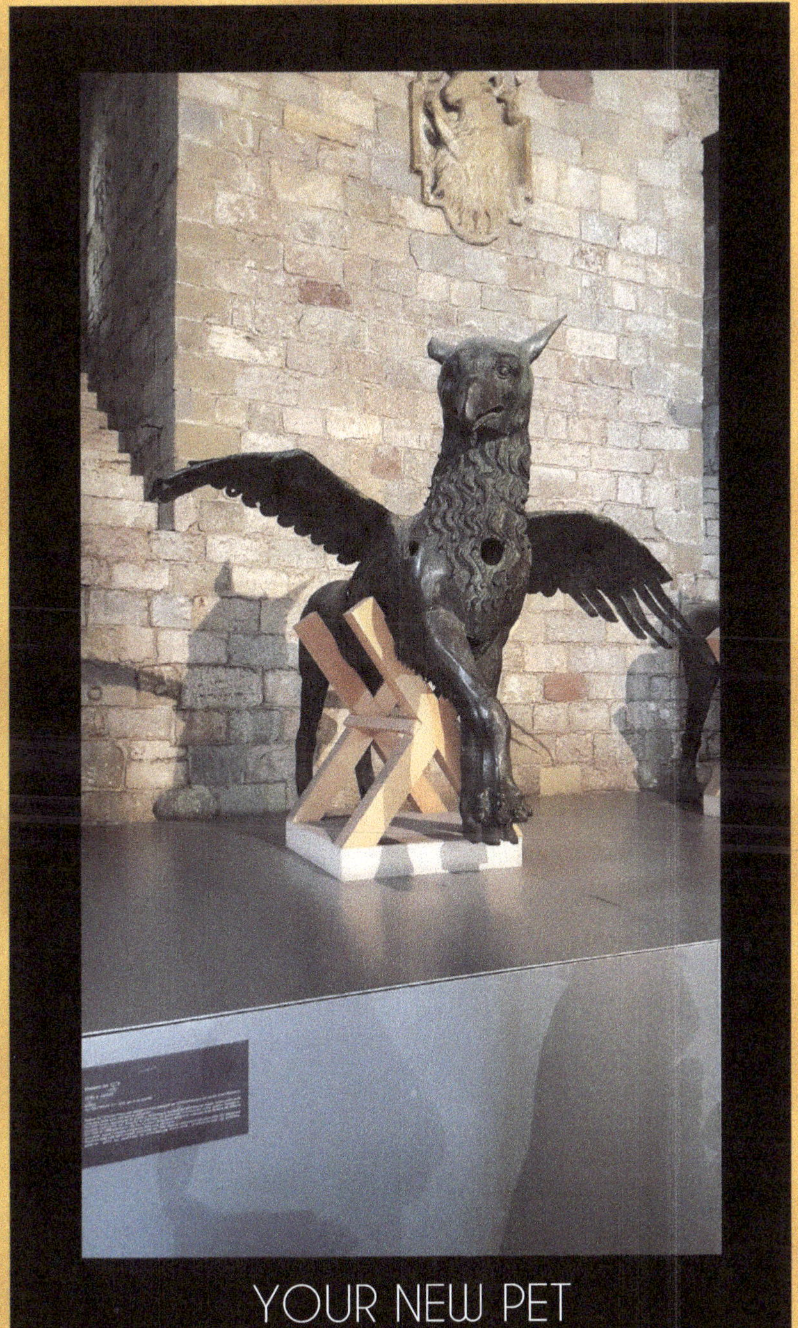

YOUR NEW PET

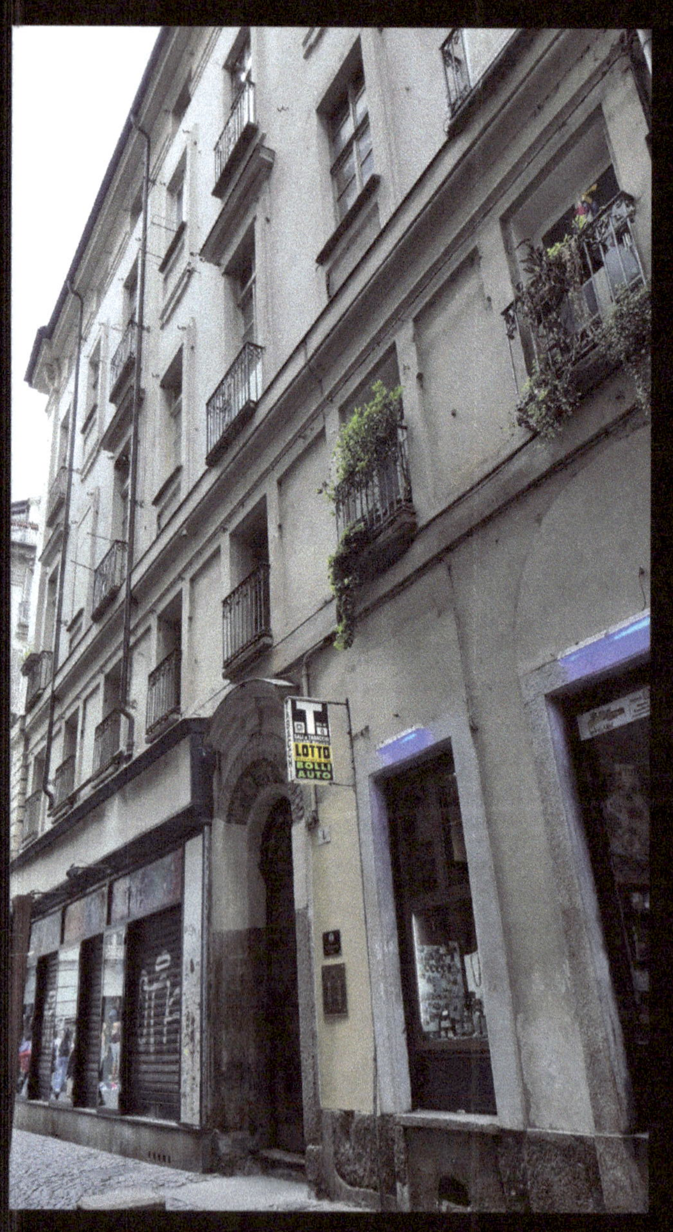

WALKING HOME

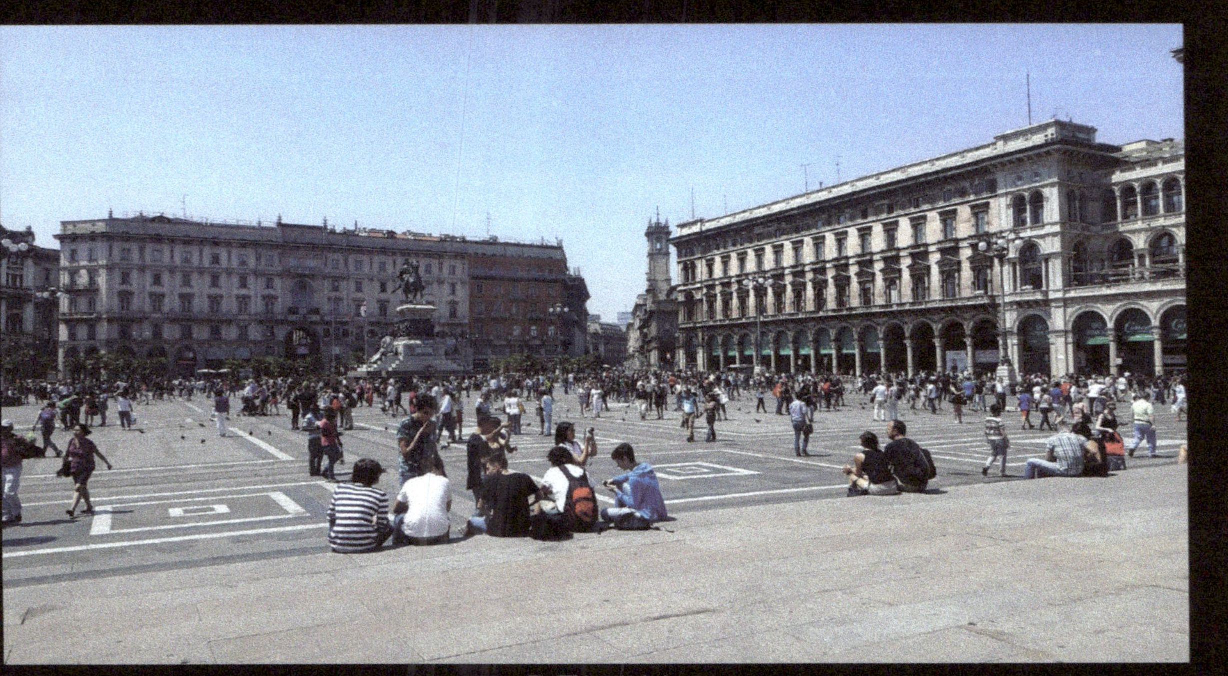
RELAX

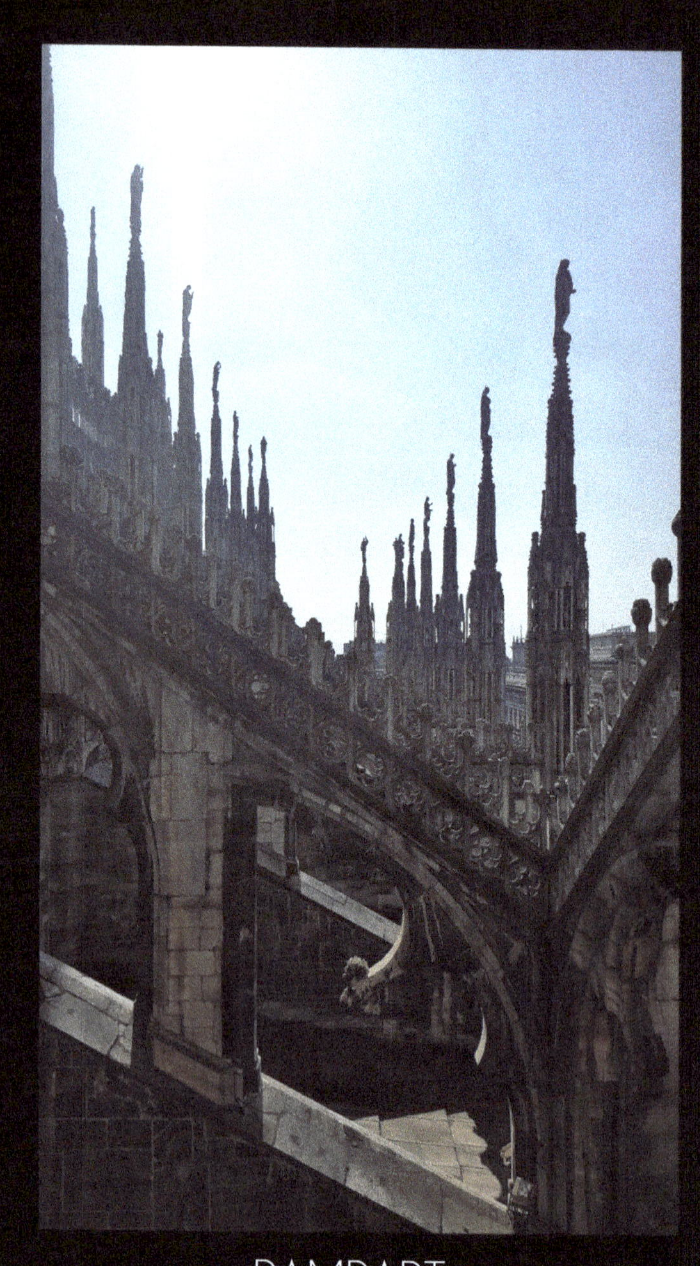

RAMPART

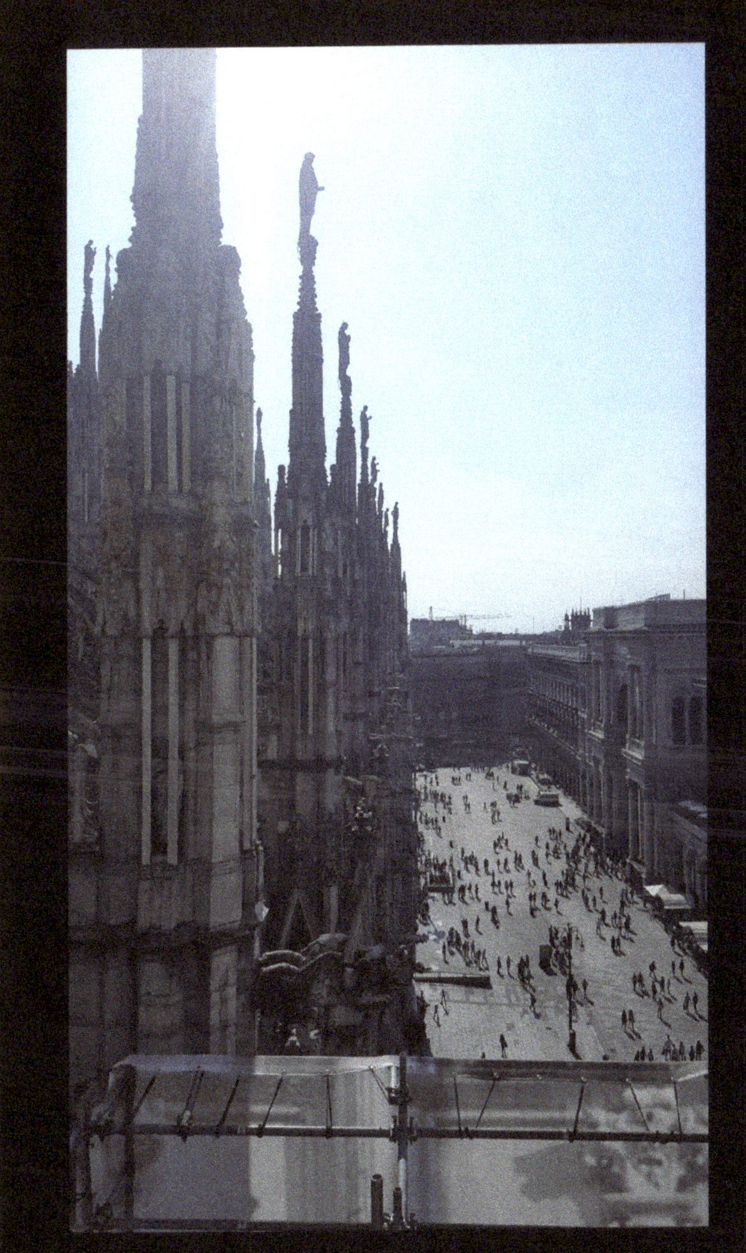

FROM ON HIGH

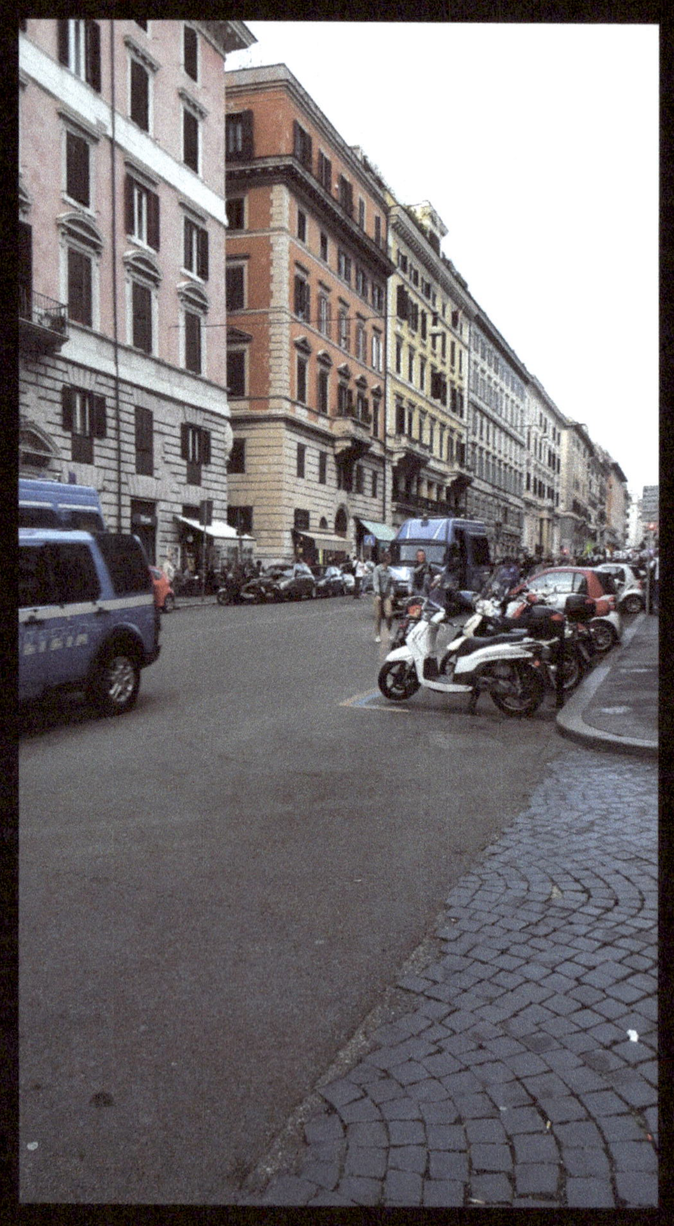

CRUISING

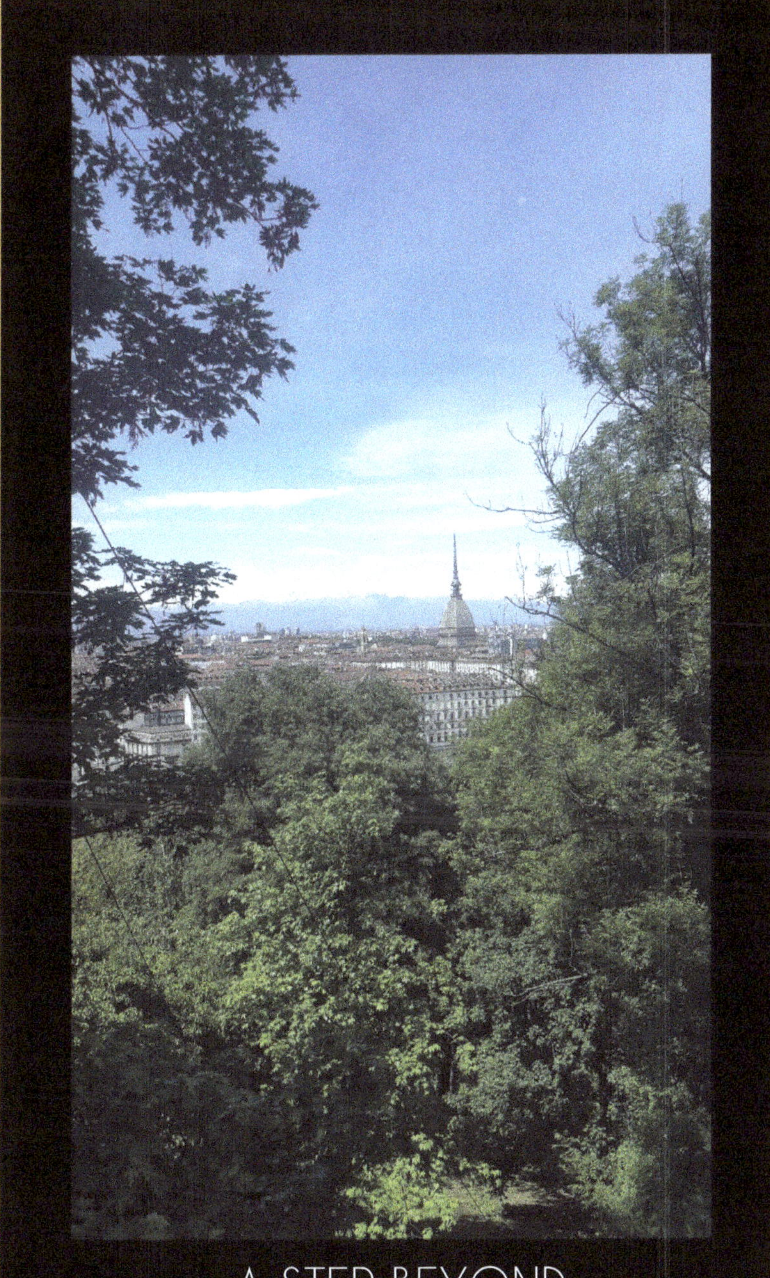

A STEP BEYOND

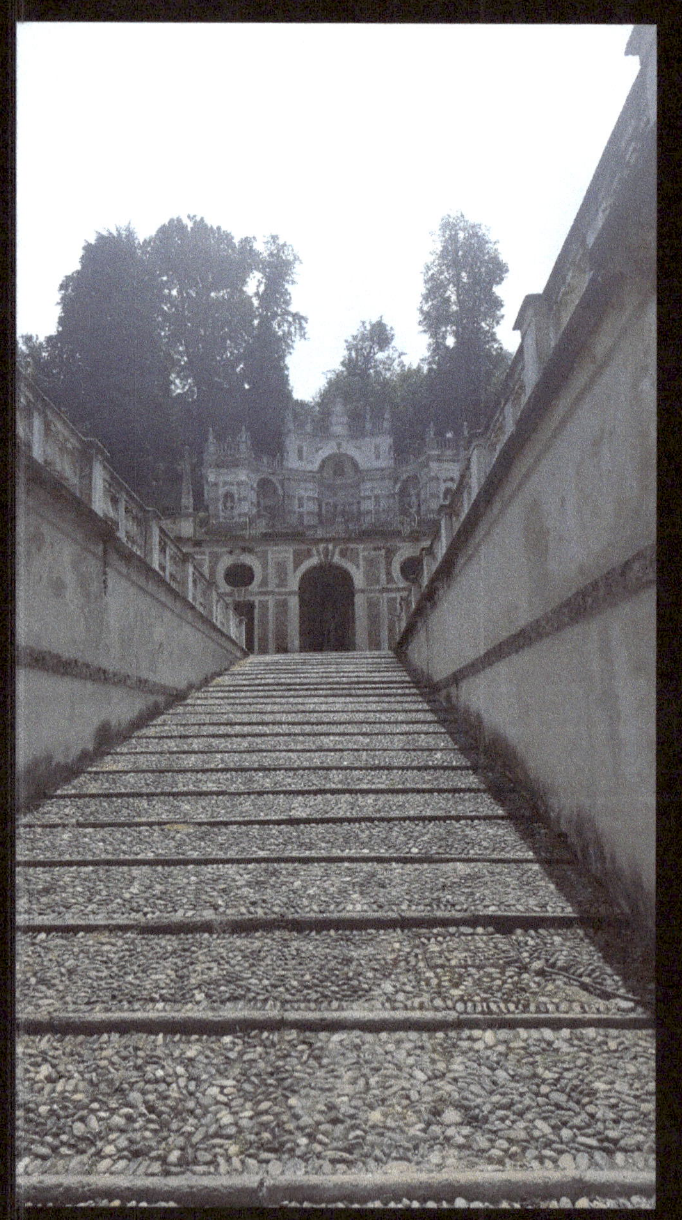

FUNNEL

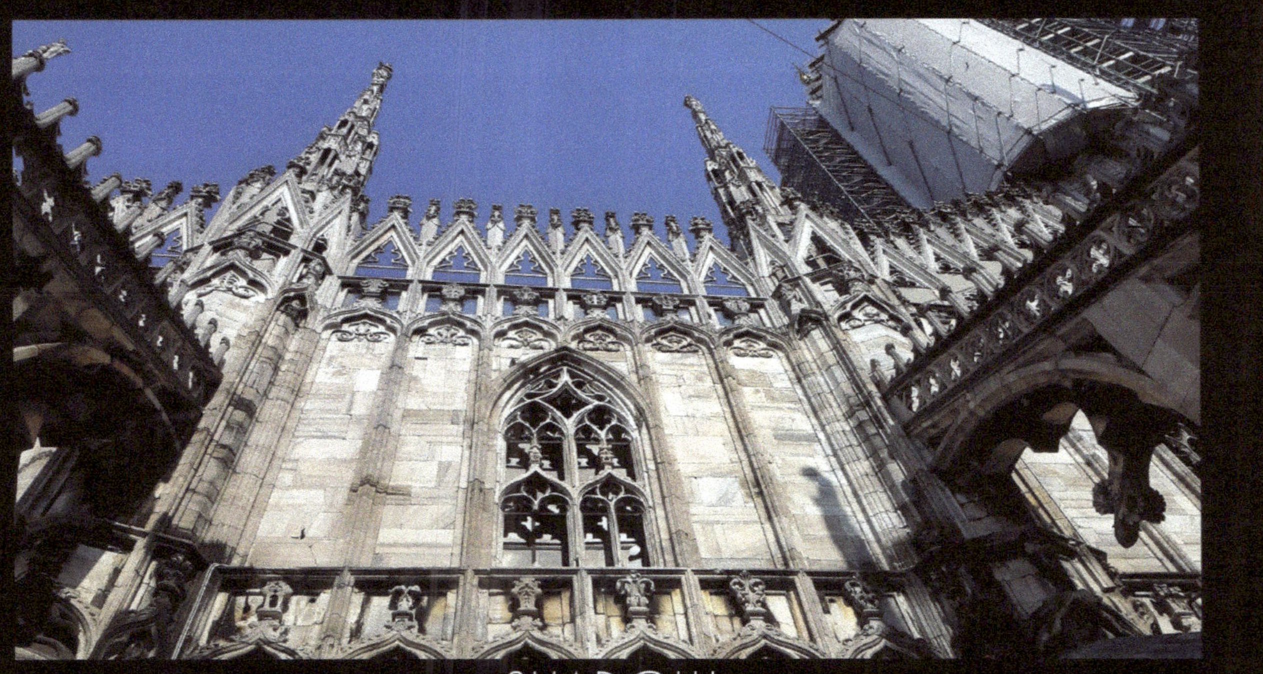
SHADOW

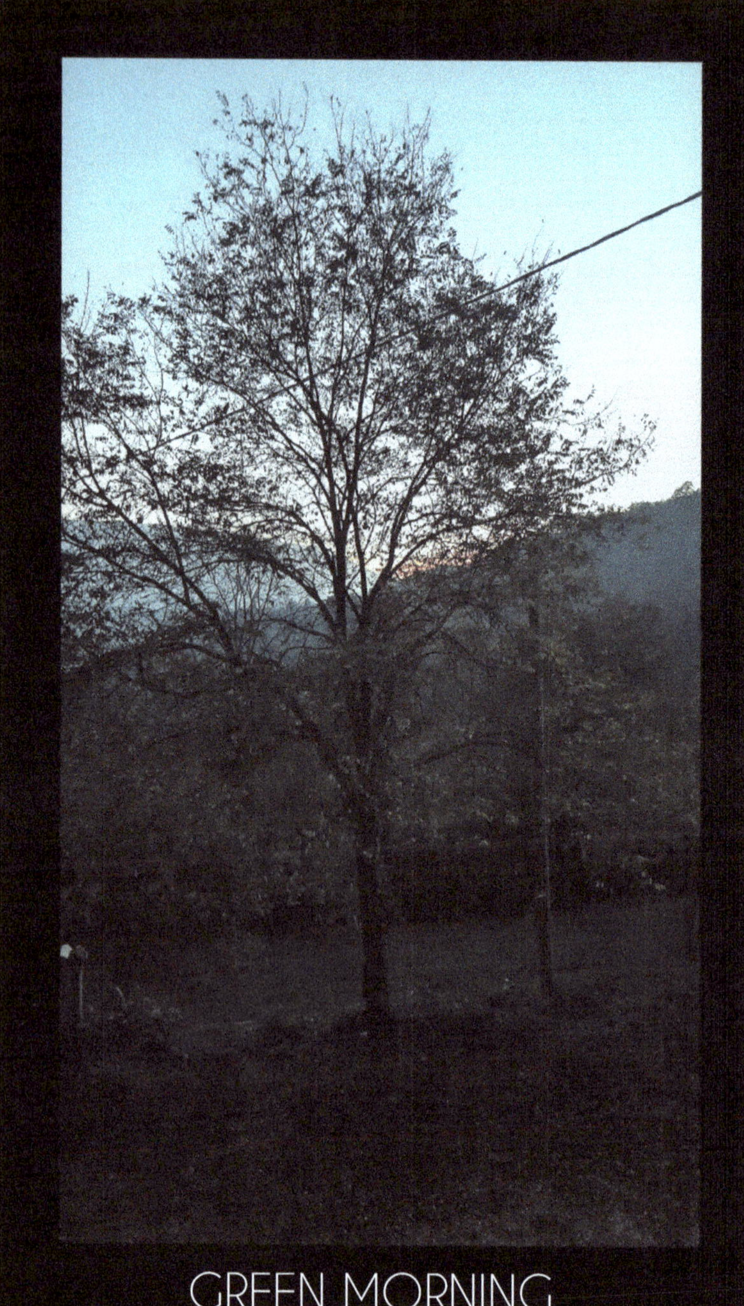

GREEN MORNING

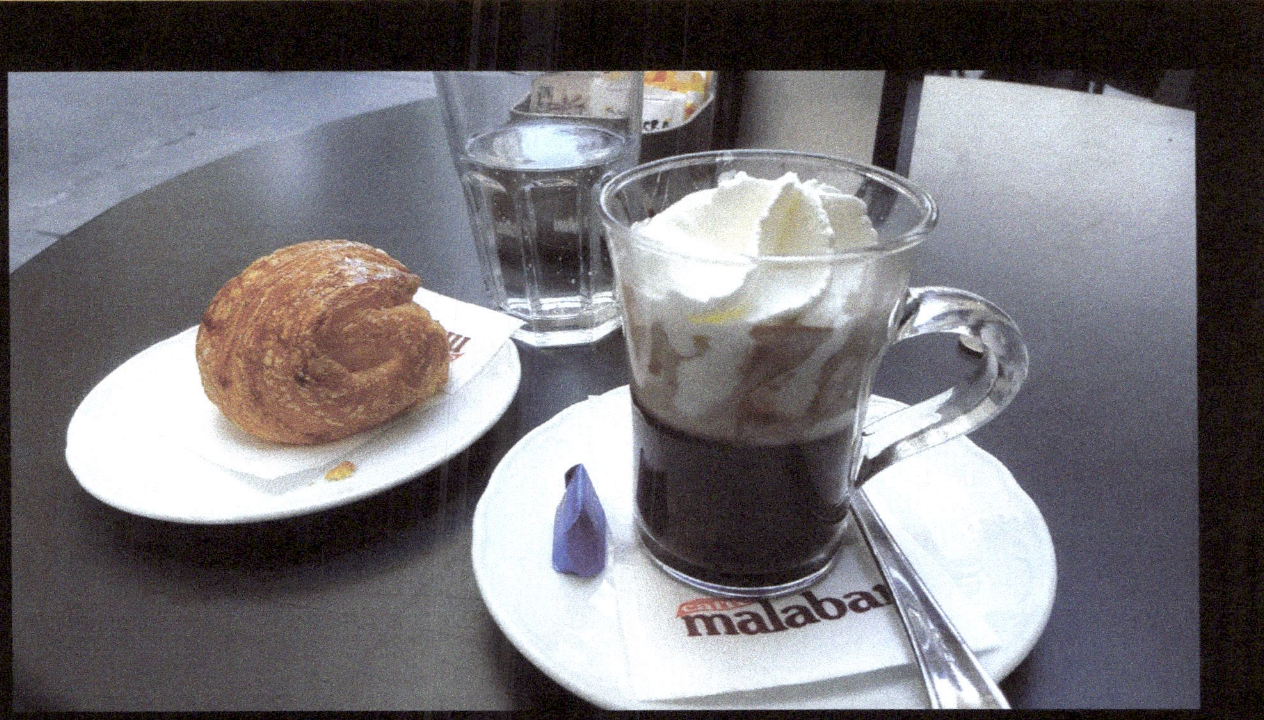

malabar
BICERIN

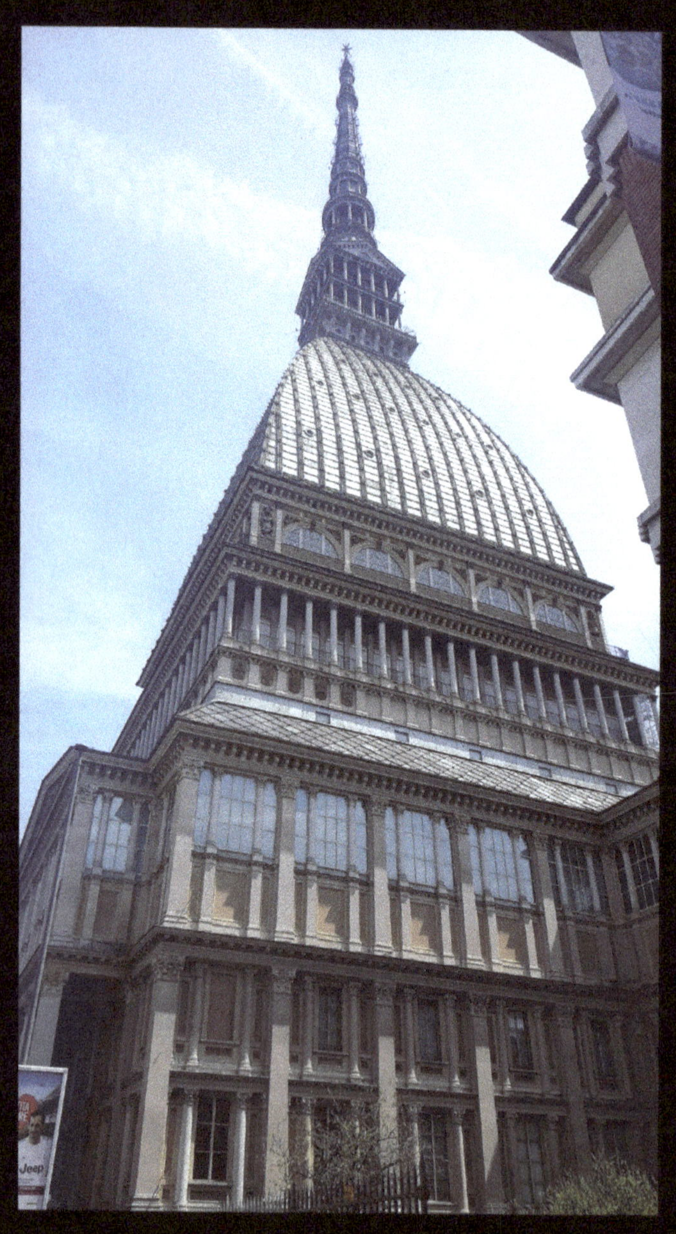

FRANKENSTEIN

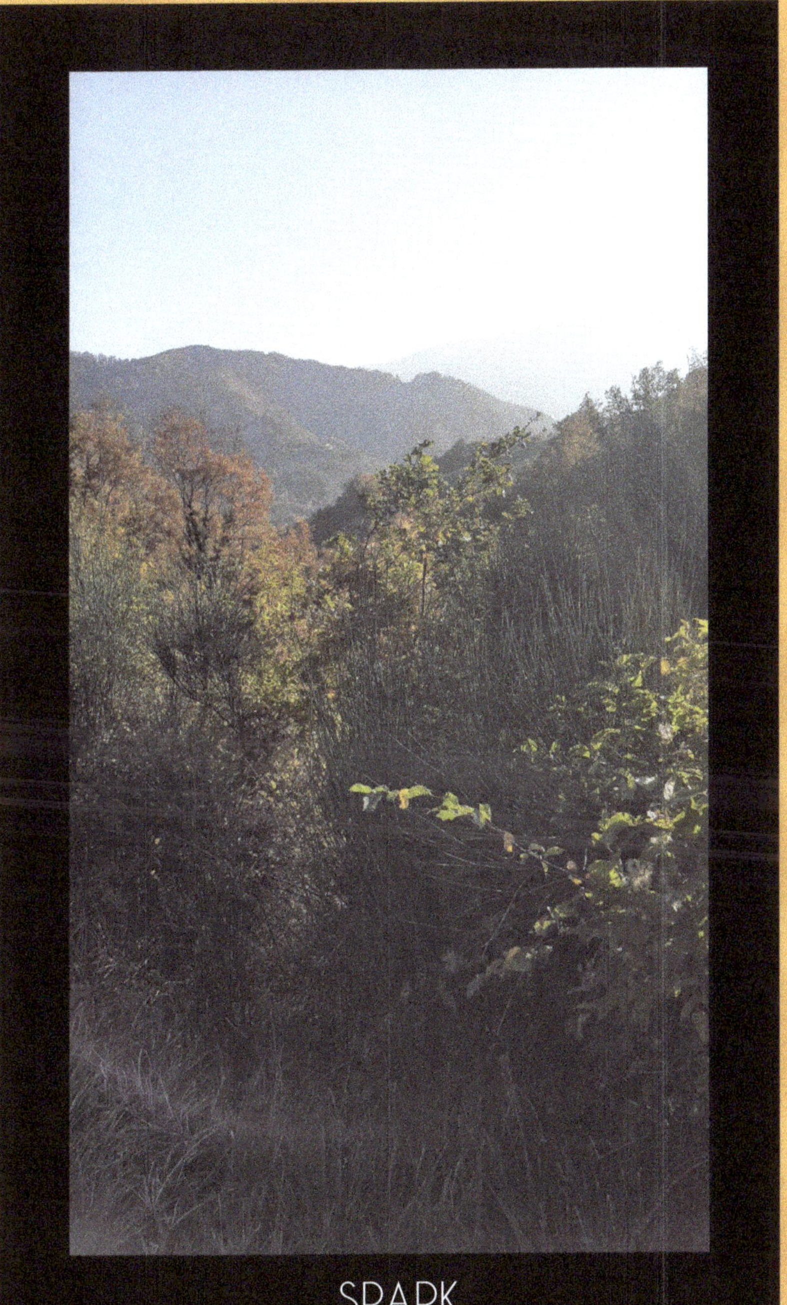

SPARK

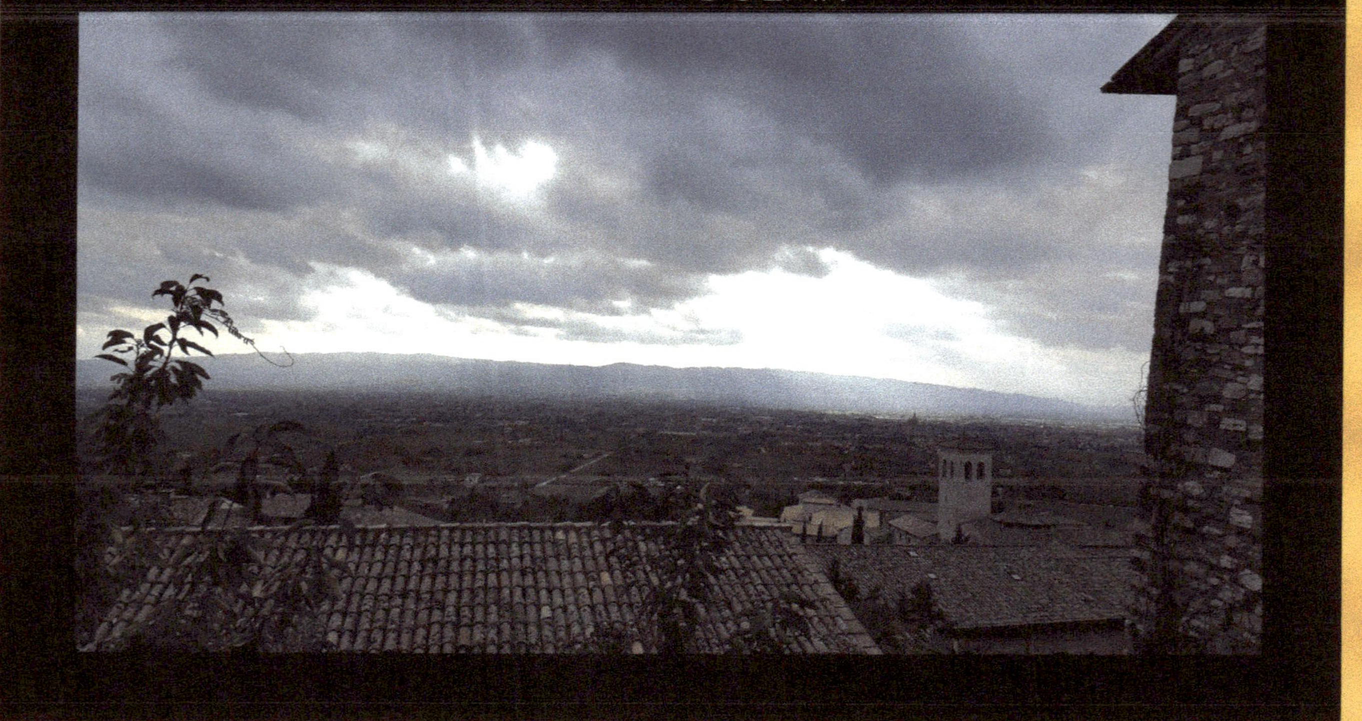
SPECTACULAR

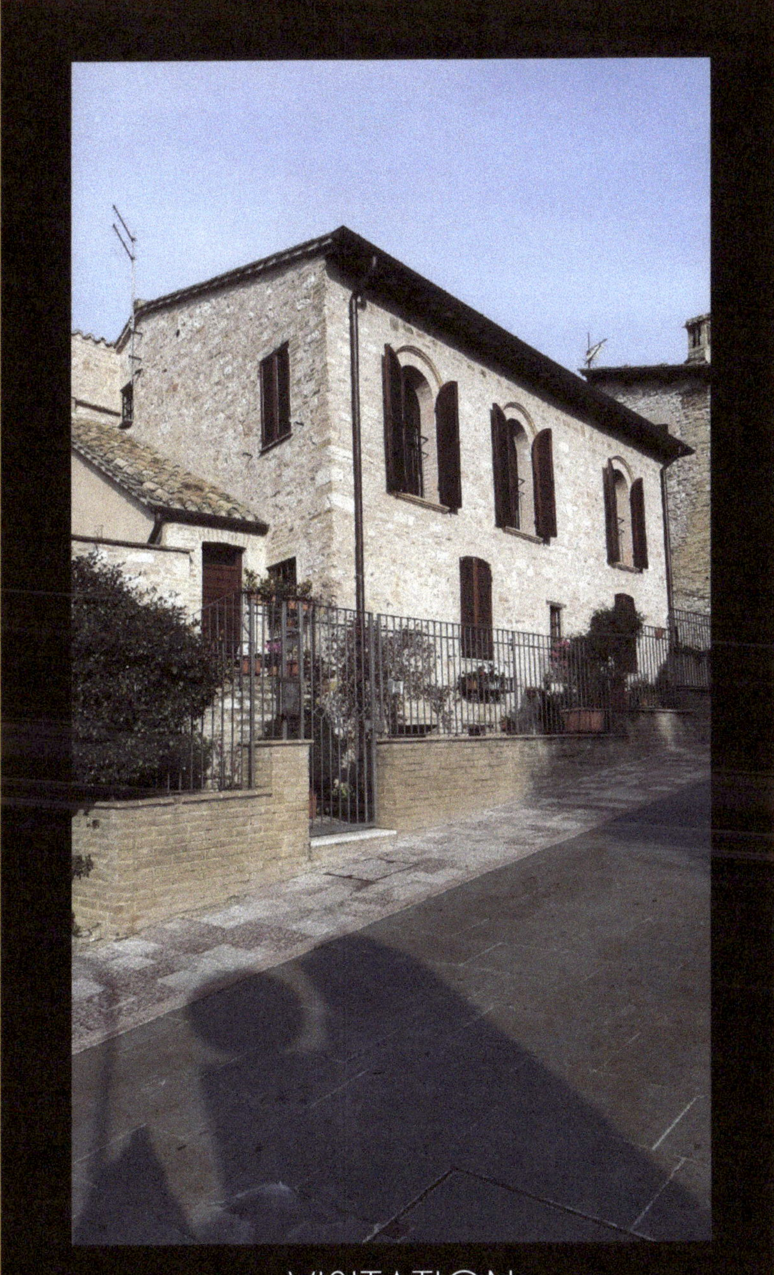

VISITATION

WIDE OPEN

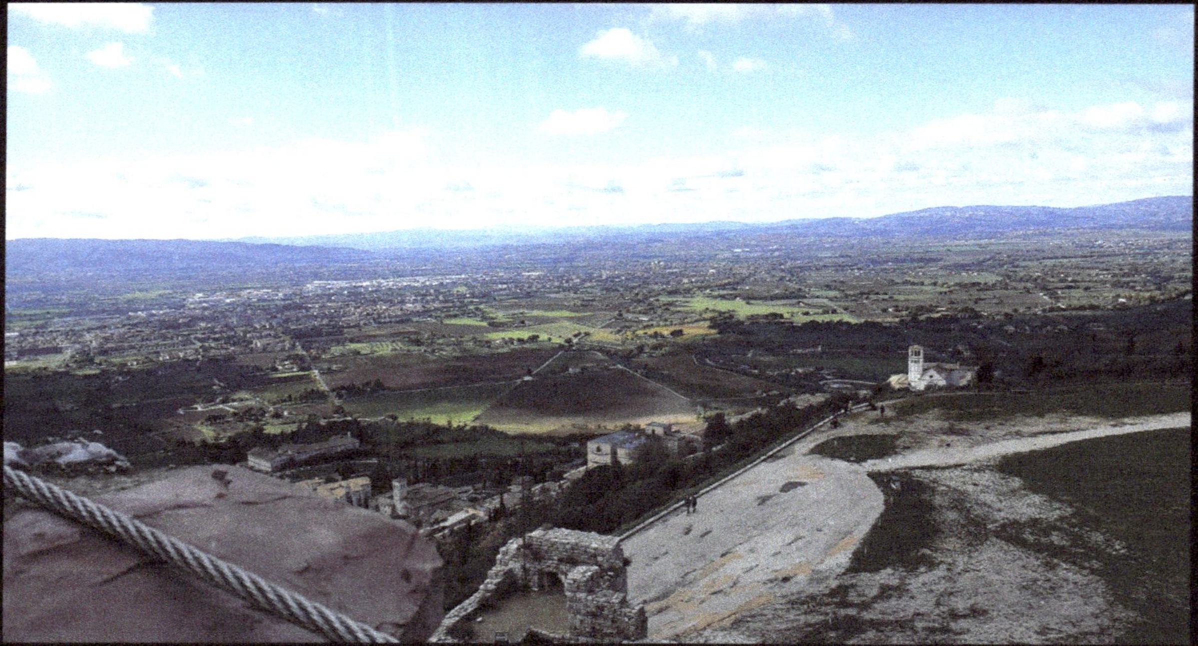

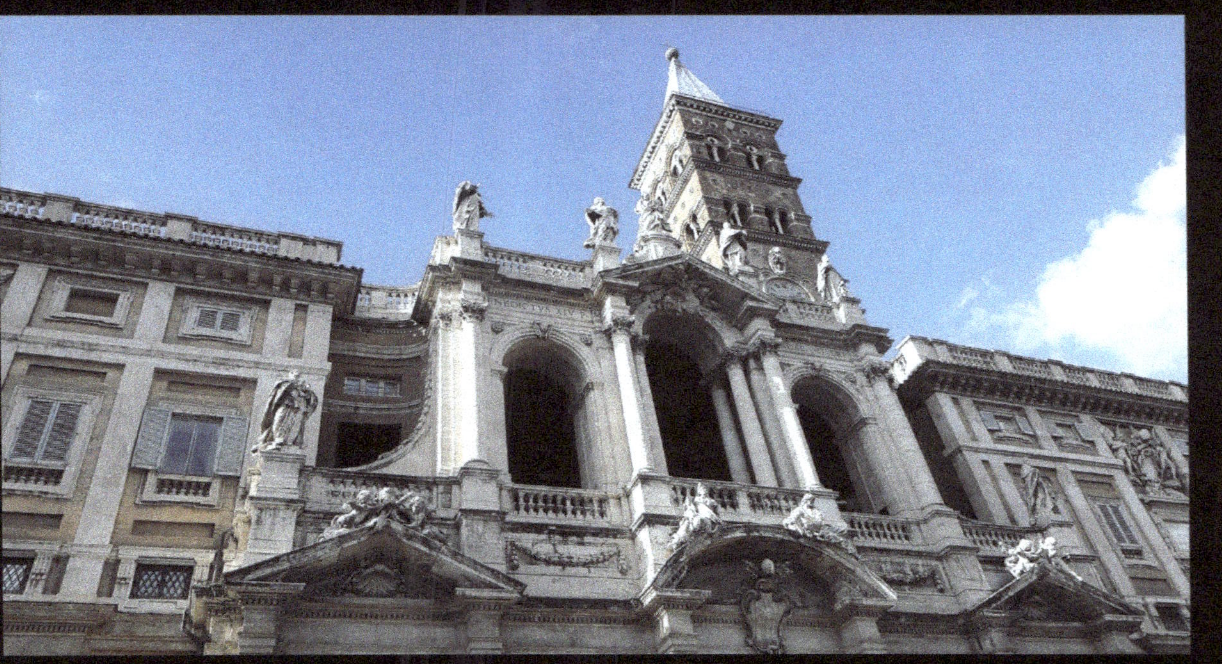

IMPOSING

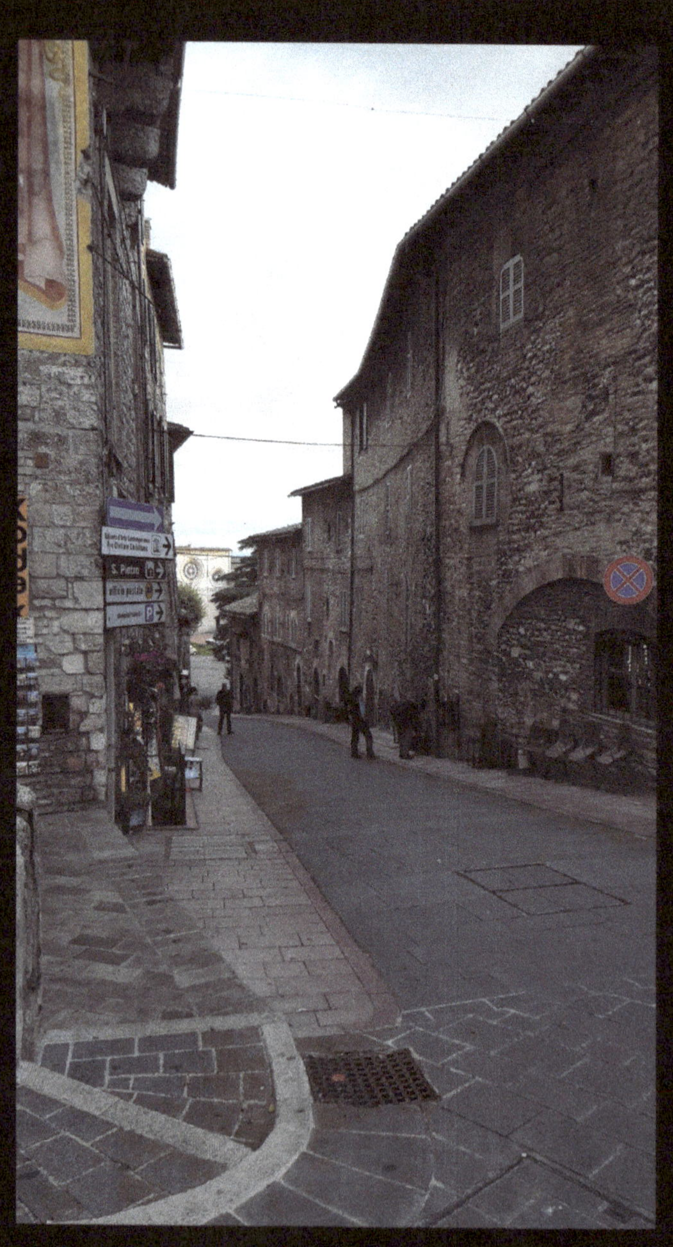

THROUGH THE MAZE

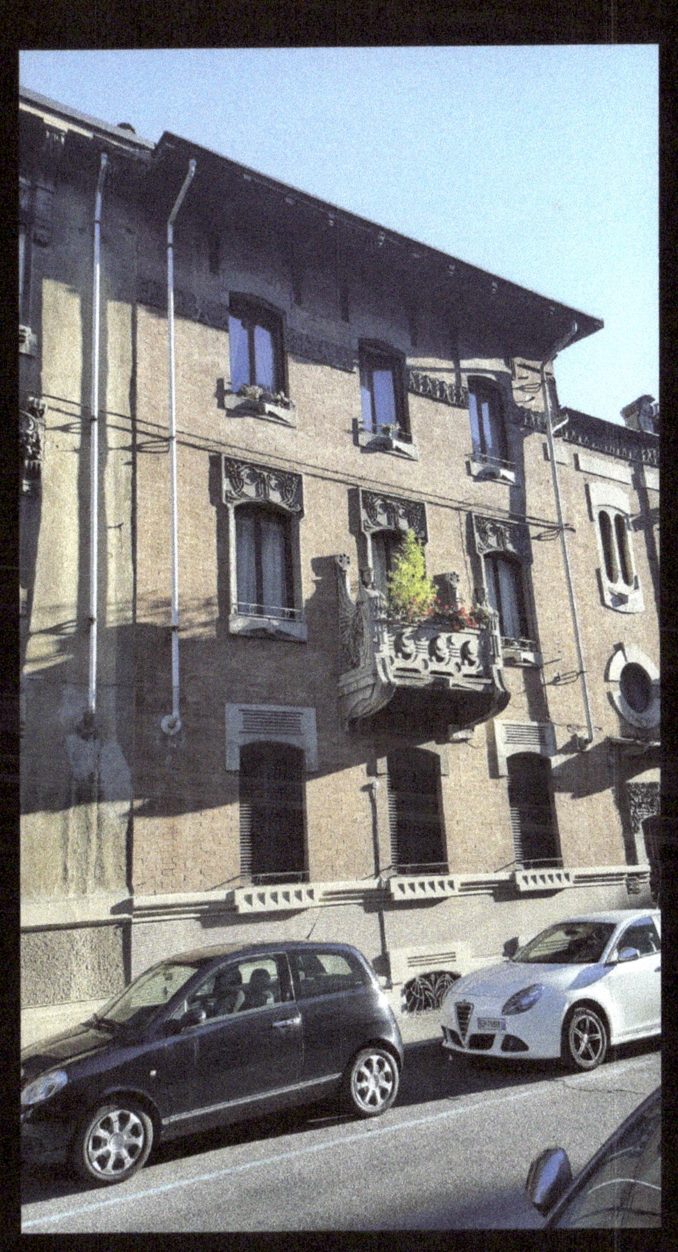

SPARK OF LIFE

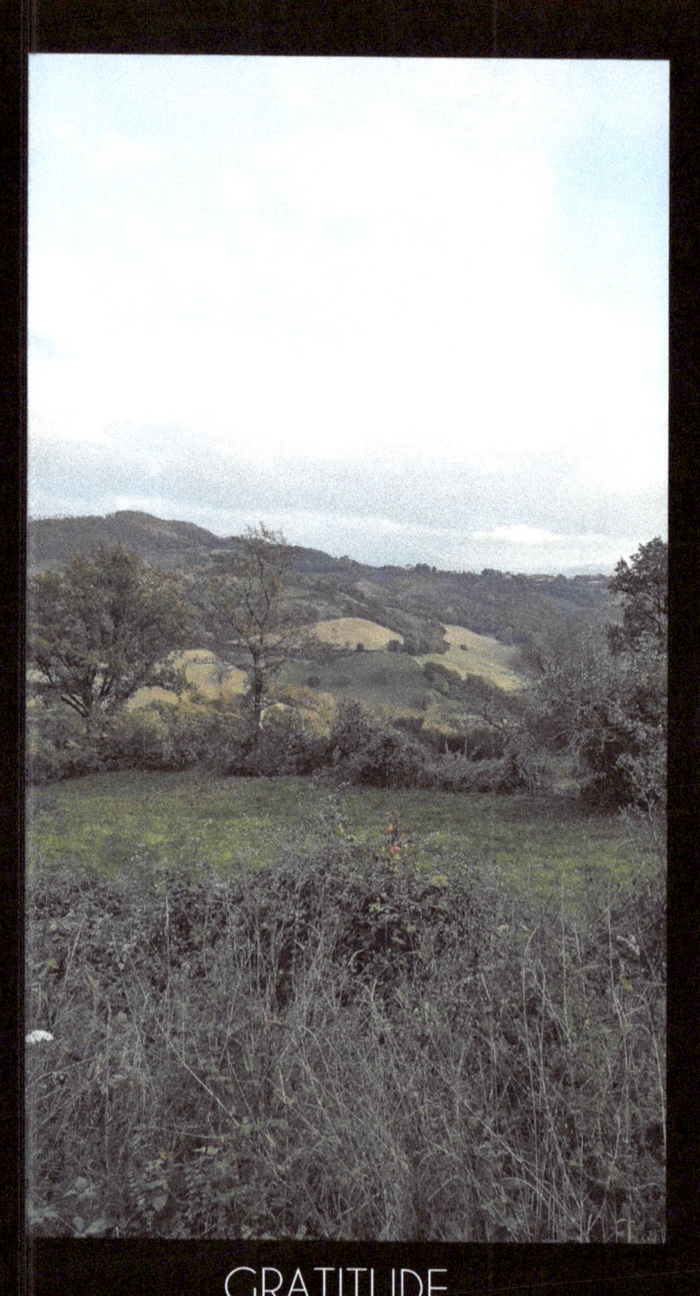
GRATITUDE

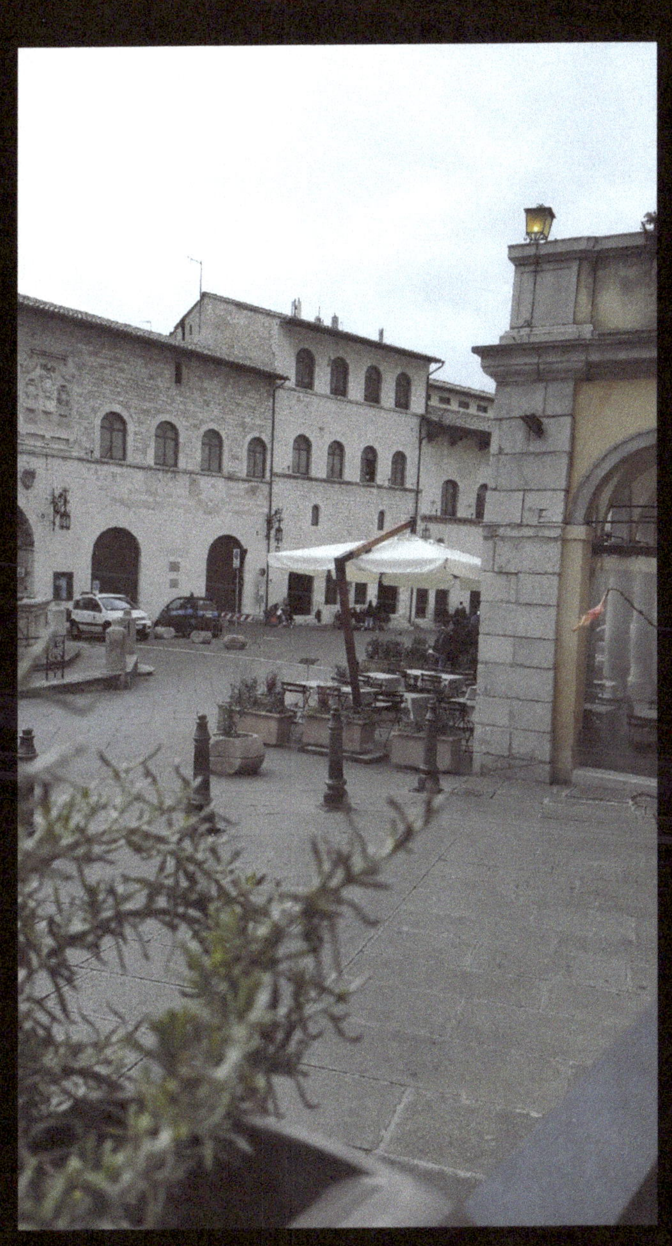

GLIMPSES

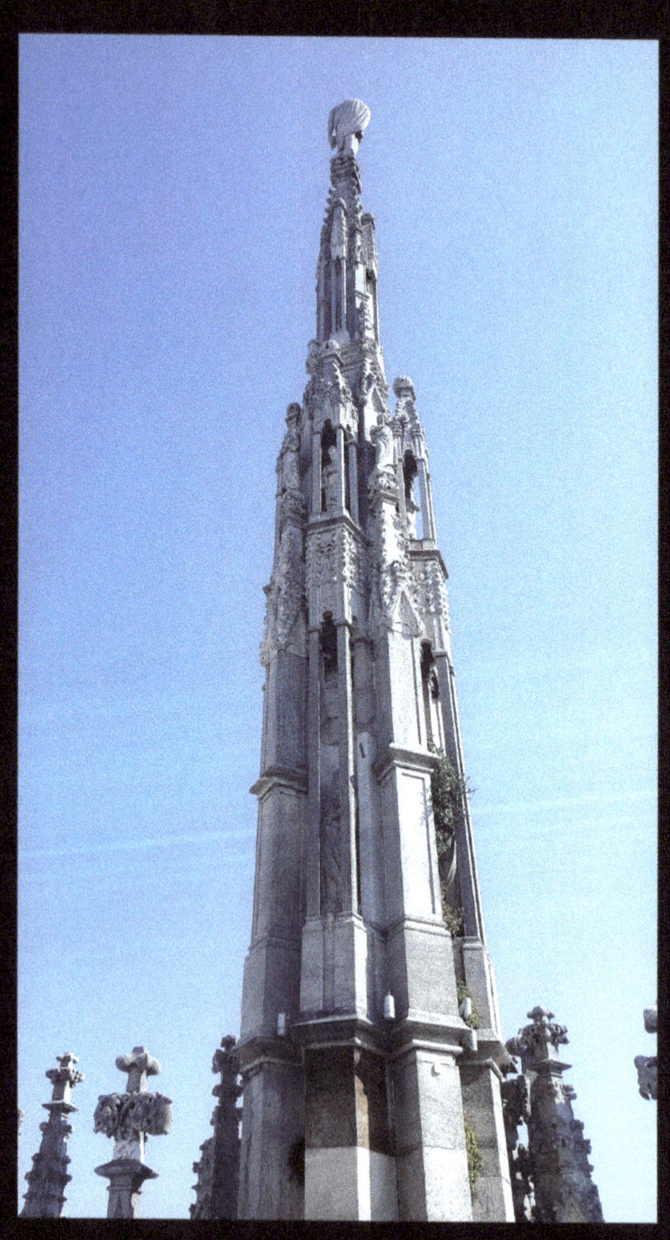

ASCEND

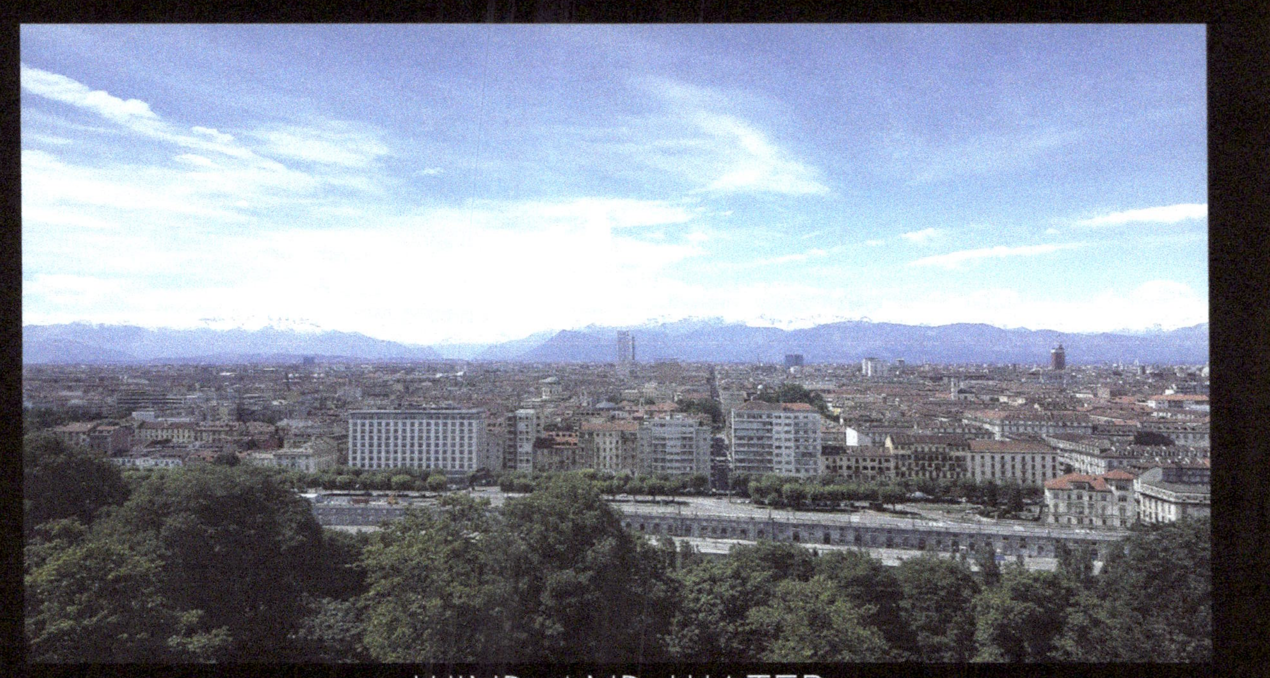
WIND AND WATER

THRUST

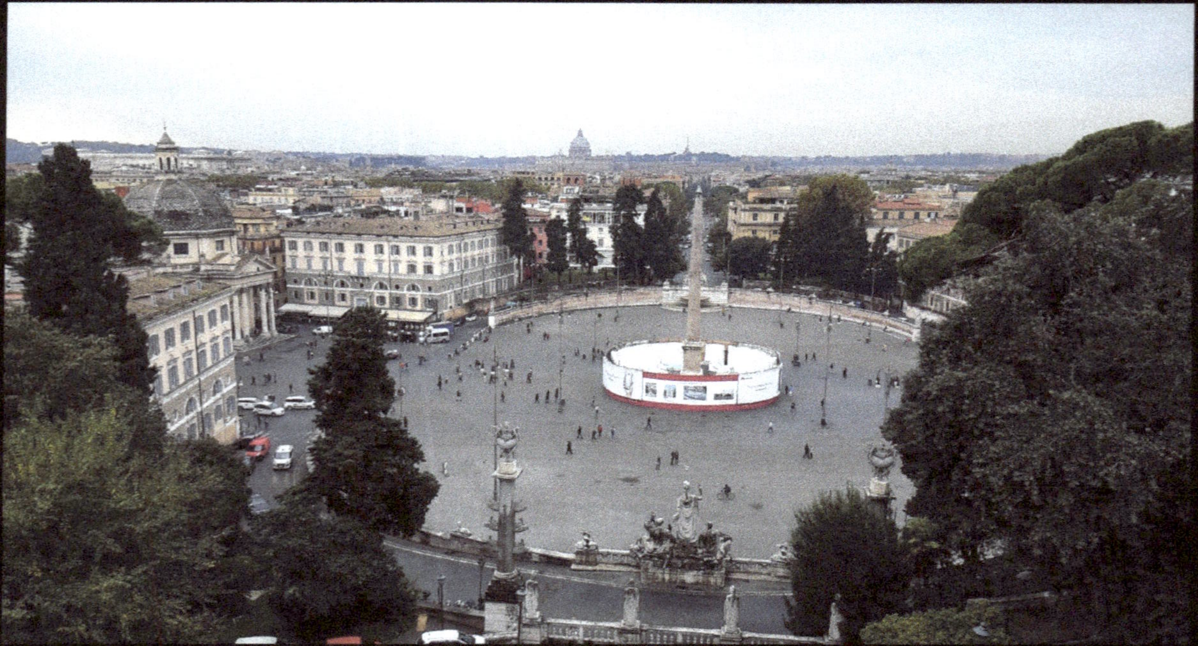

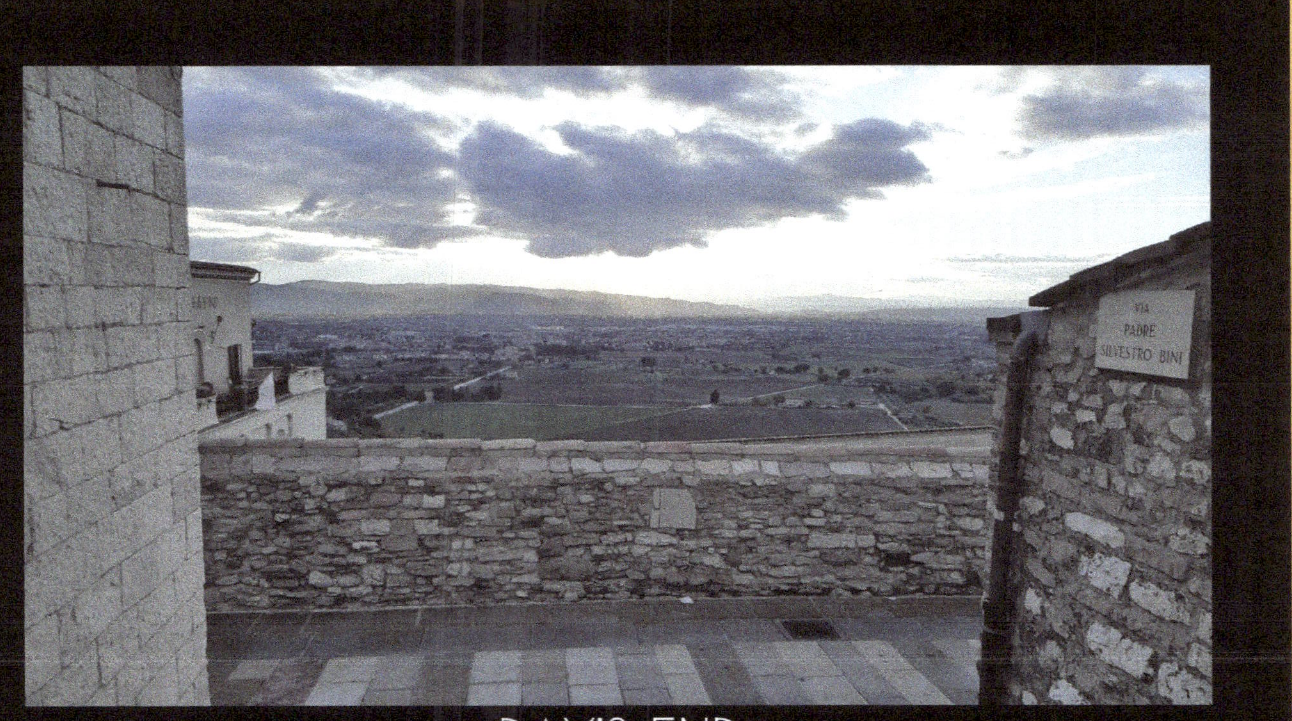

DAY'S END

About the Author

Laine Cunningham is an award-winning novelist. Her women's travel adventure memoir *Woman Alone: A Six-Month Journey Through the Australian Outback* appeals to fans of *Wild* and *Eat Pray Love*.

Fiction

The Family Made of Dust

Beloved

Reparation

Nonfiction

Woman Alone

On the Wallaby Track: Australian Words and Phrases

Seven Sisters: Messages from Aboriginal Australia

Writing While Female or Black or Gay

The Zen of Travel
The Zen of Gardening
Zen in the Stable
The Zen of Chocolate
The Zen of Dogs

The Wisdom of Puppies
The Wisdom of Babies
The Wisdom of Weddings

Bikes of Berlin
Necropolises of New Orleans I & II
Ruins of Rome I & II
Ancients of Assisi I & II
Panoramas of Portugal
Nuances of New York
Glimpses of Germany
Impressions of Italy
Utopia of the Unicorn

9 781946 732811